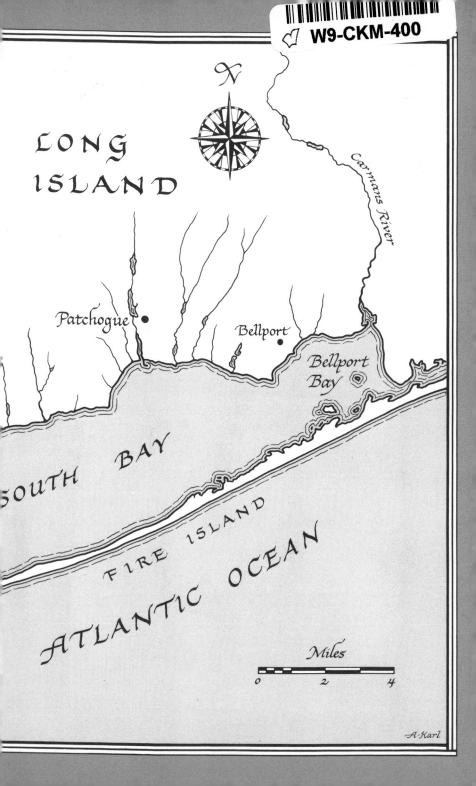

LONG
ISLAND

Patchogue

Bellport

Bellport
Bay

Carmans River

SOUTH BAY

FIRE ISLAND

ATLANTIC OCEAN

Miles

0   2   4

A·Karl

Bod   Bode, Richard
 B   Blue sloop at dawn.

BLUE SLOOP AT DAWN

BLUE SLOOP

AT DAWN

Richard Bode

275p

DODD, MEAD & COMPANY, NEW YORK

1979

1 2 3 4 5 6 7 8 9 10

Library of Congress Cataloging in Publication Data

Bode, Richard.
    Blue sloop at dawn.

    1.Bode, Richard. 2.United States—Biography.
I.Title.
CT275.B5822A33   973.91'092'4   [B]   79–1439
ISBN 0–396–07658–0

For Jeff, Keith, Tricia and Katie
"There is more day to dawn."

BLUE SLOOP AT DAWN

1

I *haven't sailed for twenty-five years, but I still can't pass*
a harbor without hearing halyards slapping in the wind.
Usually I suppress my longing, but one October day—
after dropping my daughter off at college—I drove into
a shipyard at Northport that I had passed many times
before. It was a small yard with a pier tucked between
the road and Sound, and I suddenly realized I always
took this back route home so that I might relive my
vanished youth as I sped by.

It was an innocent indulgence, and I have no idea what
compelled me to veer off the paved highway onto the
cinder road that day. Perhaps it was the nostalgic taste
of autumn in those northern puffs that swept across the
Sound from the far Connecticut shore. There's no more
venturesome season for sailing than early fall when the
fickle wind alternately gusts and fades. One minute
you're clambering up the windward deck and the next
you're flat becalmed.

I parked beside a rickety storage shed and walked between two skiffs that had been hauled up on the ways,

one to have her glass bottom scrubbed and the other to have oakum stuffed into a leaky garboard seam. A carpenter lay on his back below the older hull and each time his limber arm swung upward the hollow ping of his caulking hammer echoed across the yard. I stepped over the rails and skirted a timber brace, and then I heard a methodical wooden thump coming from the water's edge, as regular as a metronone.

If you're lucky enough to have grown up with sailboats, you never forget how they grunt and groan. Even now, after the passage of a quarter-century, I can still recognize the strains of a sloop at anchor, a sloop luffing, a sloop pointing, and a sloop running with the wind. And so, when I heard that repetitive thump, I knew at once it was an unsecured tiller rapping against the cockpit coaming as the boat swayed in the wind at her berth.

I approached the pier and a lone mast loomed before me; then I saw the slender sloop with her bow tied to a mooring post and her stern to a shorter post that protruded through the dock. As the wind blew she swung like a weathervane within the limits of her lines. The force of the water against the rudder moved the tiller as if she were in the grip of some ghostly hand. I had an irresistible itch to leap aboard and seize the wayward stick and feel the surge of wind and water rising through the rudderpost into my arm. That was a sensation I had once known but hadn't experienced for a long time.

As my gaze shifted from the tiller I was struck at once by her graceful sheer. I learned to sail in that era before the molded plastic hull, and I had a weakness for wooden boats whose planks were steamed and shaped to curve upward fore and aft so artfully. While other men dream

2

of buxom women, I dream of a sloop with flare.

"This is a sound boat," I thought to myself, "just the kind I would buy if I were in the market now." She had a protective cuddy and a utility centerboard that dropped through a leaded keel, plus a tall mast and a short boom that just cleared the aft stay. And she was a perfect size for day sailing—about 23 feet overall and perhaps 18 along the waterline.

I studied her carefully and she seemed strangely familiar. Then all at once I realized this boat was mine! This was the same boat I had once owned and sailed—not here on the Sound but on the other side of the Island amid the shoals and channels of the Great South Bay. This was a Timber Point class sloop, one of twenty-three built more than fifty years ago. I would know a Timber Point anywhere, anytime. But this wasn't just any Timber Point; this was Number 3, the third one built, the one that had belonged to me for awhile and now belonged to somebody else.

It had changed, of course. My sloop had bright decks that needed constant varnishing, while this one had been covered with canvas. My sloop had a deep blue hull—this hull was painted white. But those were superficial differences, ones that might normally occur through changes in ownership and the assaults of weather, sea, and salt. None of those alterations masked her unmistakable character. I could see she was still fit and free of rot, a testimony to those who had originally built her and those who later cared for her, including myself.

I sat down on the mooring post. The clove hitch was twisted under me and the taut stern line passed between my legs. It seemed incredible that after twenty-five years

3

I should unexpectedly loop back this way to find myself. This was my boat. I remembered when I saw her for the first time, gliding effortlessly as a swan up a south shore creek, not knowing that some day she would be mine. I remembered when my skeptical Uncle Bert had bought her for his daughter, Sara, and myself, half afraid that we couldn't handle "that hunk of machinery," as he called it. I remembered when I learned to sail, the people who taught me, and how I graduated from boat to boat. And I remembered when I first felt the seawind blowing out of the marshes and mingling with my blood.

For the first ten years of my life I was a city boy who had grown up hating city streets. The view I remember best looked westward from my parent's apartment on Riverside Drive across the Hudson River to the Palisades. Sometimes on a late spring day the south wind came out of New York Bay and blew past the Battery as far north as Ninety-Eighth Street, but by the time it reached my bedroom window it was diluted with soot.

My father was a commercial artist who worked for department stores and advertising agencies and fashion magazines. He lived in the city, he said, because he had to be near the people who hired him. But I suspect the truth was otherwise. My parents were true children of the Flapper Age who came alive after the sun went down. They took long afternoon naps so they could dance till dawn.

They danced clear through the Roaring Twenties into the Depression years that cast a pall across my boyhood. From my bedroom window I could see not only the

Jersey cliffs, but also the makeshift shanties along the near river bank—black smoke rising through roof pipes —which served as homes for the down and out. I think my mother saw them too. Now and then she would suggest that we move to the country (anyplace beyond the city limits was the country) "for Rick's sake," but my father would immediately offer a dozen reasons why this was impossible.

My mother was an affectionate, childlike woman who yielded to my father's whims. He showed her how to fix her hair, told her what to wear and how much rouge and eye shadow to put on. For some reason, my parent's friends felt obliged to inform me that my mother was "a stunning woman, a gorgeous creature," and all that sort of nonsense, as if I really cared. My mother didn't seem to me to be anything except my mother whom I loved regardless of how she looked.

My mother often modeled for my father, as I sometimes did myself. In his drawings, my father transformed us into fashion plates to promote clothing sales for Bonwit Teller and Saks Fifth Avenue. But I recall that when he finished his pencil sketches he would set a canvas on his easel and work in oils with a pallet-knife. Then he painted vivid scenes of Moorish harbors and Arabian marts. He painted white birches and the rocky ledges of the Maine coast. He painted an Indian squaw holding her papoose, both wrapped in a long red shawl. He painted out of his imagination sights he had never seen.

My favorite was a romantic painting of a lateen-rigged dhow floating across an endless sea. When I stood up close, the painting was nothing but a jumble of color, but

5

it came sharply into focus as I backed away. I often sat across the living room in my father's armchair and gazed at that painting, pretending I was aboard the vessel drifting off the coast of Africa.

In the summer, my parents packed me off to a camp in the Berkshires where the wind was landlocked. The camp was set amid those timeless hills where one feels homesick on the site. Even then I was known among my summer friends as something of a "loner." I would wander by myself along the trails, deep into the woods, sit between the exposed roots of a gleaming beech tree and watch for the dart of a stray animal.

The camp was a refuge from the paved playgrounds in that grimy city my parents refused to leave. I longed for the camp all winter and I left it each August in sorrow. Unlike many of the other children, I didn't cry upon leaving for the summer that would never come again. I merely said a silent farewell to the lake and hills and trees.

When I left that camp for the last time it wasn't late August but mid-July. It was on my tenth birthday, to be precise, and I was expecting my parents to visit me. They were late, as usual, and I decided to bide my time by rowing on the lake. I had spent considerable effort learning to row that summer, and I could now move the boat in either direction with clean, bold strokes. I had even mastered the technique of driving the boat forward with one oar and backward with the other, thereby turning it sharply on its own axis. I was especially proud of this feat, and I hoped that when my parents finally arrived they would stroll down to the lake, see me maneuvering across the water, and admire my new-found prow-

6

ess and skill. Every now and then I would glance over my shoulder toward shore to see if they were standing there, watching their son. But they didn't come.

The morning sun climbed slowly up the sky and the faint breeze died, and still they didn't come. Toward noon, I saw my counsellor standing on the dock, gravely waving me ashore. When I landed, he took the bow line and told me I had a visitor. "A visitor?" I said. I thought it strange he should use so vague a term when he knew I was expecting my parents. He nodded, and his solemn manner sent a shiver along my spine.

I threw a towel across my shoulders, for I had suddenly turned cold. I walked to the camp director's office and found Uncle Bert waiting there. "Let's take a walk, Rick," he said. We headed together down a trail and he told me what I had already guessed. He said my parents had been killed in an auto accident the night before while driving up to visit me. He said he would help me pack my things. He said I was coming home now to live with him.

I still can't talk at length about the silent trip out of those darkening hills. I recall the gathering storm but I know it didn't rain. I let myself go numb. It was far better, I thought, to feel nothing at all than to succumb to bitterness and pain.

It was after midnight when we arrived at Uncle Bert's bungalow in Bay Shore. We had driven a great distance, most of it through darkness, but as soon as we crossed a large bridge I felt the change in air. To my mind, there are two worlds. One lies in the mountains and the other at the shore. I associate the former with the sweet aroma that follows rain and the latter with the pungent scent of the tidal marsh where mother-life began. The one is high and dry and the other dense and shrouded in fog.

As we pulled into the short driveway, a sense of place came back to me. During the drive home (for I think of it as "home" now) I had been trying to remember what Uncle Bert's place looked like, but I couldn't summon a clear picture even though I had been there before on several family occasions. I had a dim memory of a small one-story house surrounded by woods and that was all. I had only one sharp image, and that was of Sara, who was two years older, pushing me on a lopsided swing suspended from a tree limb in the backyard. I kept falling off and Aunt Flo kept rushing out of the house, brushing me off, and scolding Sara for pushing me too high and hard. She didn't seem to understand very much about children, and she had a mortal dread of dirty knees.

We parked under a portico that extended from the front door over the driveway. As I stepped from the car I saw in the yellow light a large sign tacked to the screen. It read: "Welcome home, Rick!" Sara, who had obviously drawn the sign, was already asleep.

Aunt Flo, however, was awake in bed with a migraine headache that always came upon her whenever a crisis arose. As I entered the front door, I heard her wavering voice calling from her sickbed: "Wipe your feet! Wipe your feet!" I'm not sure that's what she meant to say at all. But Aunt Flo was a demon housekeeper. She expressed affection by contantly cleaning, and she went out of her way to let her husband, daughter and nephew know she had performed these duties expressly for them.

"Duty" was a pivotal word in Aunt Flo's vocabulary, and she used it like a rapier. When I went in to see her in her fetid sickroom, she said that she "would do her duty by me, for I was her dear, dead sister's son." For a fleeting moment I saw my vibrant mother, now gone, and compared her with this sickly woman, still alive. I couldn't accept the fact that they were sisters, and I suddenly understood why they saw so little of each other through the years. They were different women from different worlds. While my mother was dancing on tabletops in night clubs, Aunt Flo was scrimping and saving in the country, scrubbing her kitchen floor to the point where you were scared to walk on it.

A small woman, she lay on her back in the double bed, her head sunk in the pillow down. I could barely see her, for even the faintest light hurt her eyes. She had just enough strength to tell me what to do, and no more. I thought that she too might die soon. I was still too young to know that people like her, with chronic illnesses, often have the seeds of longevity in their bones. They live to a ripe old age, complaining all the way.

"I've fixed a bed on the back screen porch," she said. "You can sleep there. When you wake up in the morning, don't make any noise. Sara will make breakfast if I'm not well. There's an extra blanket in the hall closet if you get cold."

So it was—she had looked after all the amenities. I can honestly say that in following years Aunt Flo kept her word: she did her duty by me. I never lacked for food, shelter and clothes. I was never in physical need. Perhaps it's cruel of me to suggest I received no more. Maybe the fault was mine. I didn't want to be consoled.

I erected a wall between myself and those who wanted to touch me in some tender way.

That night I lay on the porch and vowed never to let myself love anyone again. To love was to risk more than I could bear to lose. I listened to the mournful chirp of the crickets, the plaintive call of the whippoorwill. Toward dawn nature stopped and I fell asleep.

My first step in my new home was to put sufficient distance between myself and Aunt Flo, Uncle Bert and Sara. It wasn't difficult to do.

When Aunt Flo wasn't sick in bed, she was busy banging pots and pans or running errands or charging back to the grocery story to pick up something she forgot the first trip. She meticulously made out long shopping lists, but she always neglected to purchase the essential item she needed right away.

We ate supper punctually every night at seven, after Uncle Bert got off the train, but she was still struggling with the dinner dishes at half-past nine. Uncle Bert, dozing in the living room, would call in to her: "C'mon Flossie, call it quits. It's another day." Then he would look at Sara and me and ask: "What's she doing in there, anyhow?" as if he didn't know. "Fussy Flossie," he called her, but never so she'd hear.

Aunt Flo couldn't resist scribbling reprimands and leaving them about the house, especially for me. Those notes cropped up everywhere—tacked to door jambs, stuck to metal surfaces, inserted in handy crevices. They reminded me to close the refrigerator door, keep my fingers off the woodwork, turn out the closet light and, most important, not to squeeze the toothpaste from the top. At first these messages irked me, but I soon found them easy to ignore. I know I tried hard not to burst the toothpaste tube by squeezing it from the wrong end, but occasionally I forgot and discovered the earth continued to turn on its axis exactly as before. The secret to survival with Aunt Flo was to act as though she wasn't there.

As for Uncle Bert, he was also easy to avoid mainly because he was rarely around. He had two complementary traits—industry and generosity—and they conspired to keep him busy all the time. Now that he was providing for two children instead of one, he had to work twice as hard. And he did so without a murmur.

Uncle Bert left the house in Bay Shore at six-thirty every morning and returned twelve hours later. He was among that early breed of hardy commuters who sacrificed up to four hours a day traveling between their homes and their jobs. I'm sure those daily jaunts took their toll, but he never seemed the worse for wear. A meticulous man, he always appeared well-scrubbed and slightly cherubic as he stepped off the evening train. The only thing that disturbed him was the soot from the steam locomotive in the summer. "If you open the windows," he would say, "the filth pours in. And if you don't, you roast alive."

I compared his self-sacrificing nature with that of my father, who would never give up the convenience of his city apartment to undergo such an ordeal. Why did Uncle Bert do it? He did it, he said, because he wanted to raise his family where there was plenty of sunshine and fresh air.

The truth is that Uncle Bert preferred the country life himself. He seemed to be two totally different men. Dressed in a business suit, he was the typical brusk executive. But dressed in a sweatshirt and old slacks, he was the weekend gardener who liked to loaf in the sun.

On Saturday afternoons, he packed Sara and me into the back seat of his Ford coupe and drove us to Freistadts, the drug store in the heart of Bay Shore. Uncle Bert didn't drink and he didn't smoke and he didn't swear. But he had a certain weakness: a sweet tooth. The Saturday afternoon ice cream soda was as essential to his existence as the endless train ride.

What Uncle Bert actually did for a living, I had no idea for a long time. He ran something called a mortgage guarantee and title company from which he eked a meager livelihood during the Depression years. Gradually I came to understand that his business had something to do with buying and selling property. But in 1938, when I moved into the bungalow in Bay Shore, the real estate outlook was bleak indeed.

Yet I know the thought of money never entered Uncle Bert's head when he told me so firmly that tragic day that I was to come home now and live with him. From that moment he treated me—to the extent that I would let him—as if I were his son. More than anything else, he wanted me to be a brother to Sara, and Sara to be a sister to me. I think we both wanted that too.

Sara was obsessed with bumble bees. Our small house was set on a half-acre plot, surrounded by piney woods, and try as he might Uncle Bert couldn't keep the clover from taking root on his sandy lawn. In mid-July the dense white flowerheads were the favorite haunts of huge black and yellow bees.

Sara had a collection of mason jars with holes punched in the lids for air. Each morning, when the grass was still wet with dew, we'd play the stalking game she taught me. We'd move stealthily across the lawn until we spied a marauding bee buzzing about a clover head. Then, taking turns, we would slip the jar over the flower, once we were sure the bee had settled there.

As soon as the bee realized he was captured, he would fly toward light; that is, toward the bottom of the upsidedown jar. While he strove desperately to escape his glass prison, we would clasp the lid over the mouth of the jar. Then we'd add the captive to our collection on the back screen porch, where he would survive for perhaps a day, alienated from his natural world.

It was a melancholy sport for me. The excitement of the hunt didn't offset the cruelty of the capture. The bee was trapped by a fate he couldn't comprehend. We were mean and minor gods who had the power to set him free if we chose. But we looked on from afar as the bee struggled valiantly and vainly to return to the clover patch he knew. There was no going back. He was doomed to spend the rest of his life in a container, sealed off from the white and scented flowers.

One day I said to Sara: "I don't think I'm going to capture any more bees."

"All right," she said, "let's go tickle the old lady again." Tickling the old lady was also a favorite sport of Sara's.

There was another person in the bungalow when I

13

arrived, although she was only there for a short time. She was Uncle Bert's mother, Bessie Mann, who had suffered a stroke that had left her with barely enough motion in one arm to lift a spoon to her lips. Speechless, she shuffled back and forth across the living room when she wasn't sitting in her armchair, staring at a blank wall.

Whenever Sara and I were home alone (which was fairly often, since Aunt Flo was always off on an errand), Sara would seize the opportunity to go into the living room and tickle her hapless grandmother. She would run her fingers lightly down the poor old woman's belly or across the soles of her stocking feet. The tears would stream down Grandma Bessie's face and her head would drop back in a noiseless laughter that conveyed her agony. I participated in the torture once, and I shall never forget the way the tormented woman glowered at me afterward. It wasn't just the senseless tickling. She seemed to know I was the intruder who had come to dislodge her from her only home.

"I know, I know," her burning eyes seemed to say, "that soon enough my son will send me to a nursing home to make room for you."

And that's exactly what happened. Uncle Bert sent his mother away, and I know he never forgave himself for forsaking her. But it really wasn't all my fault. Aunt Flo had already made it plain that, for all her sense of duty, she couldn't take care of both her sister's son and her husband's mother at the same time.

"No," I said to Sara, "I really don't feel much like tickling the old lady either."

"Well," she said, "if you don't want to trap bees and

you don't want to tickle the old lady, what do you want to do?"

"Let's catch frogs," I said.

The dismal swamp was four blocks away. It was populated with ugly, croaking frogs who gazed at you through bulbous eyes from behind saturated leaves or under partially sunken logs. On my first visit to the swamp, I had been afraid to grab one of these warty, tailless creatures. When I reached out, they would leap away. Sara goaded me on. She was fearless when it came to bees and scared witless when it came to frogs, but she wanted me to take one home and keep it in a box where she could poke and prod it. "Go ahead, Rick!" she whispered. "There's one, grab it!" To prove my manliness, I yanked one out of the water and stuffed it in my pocket. But before we left the swamp, I secretly let it go. When Sara discovered my treachery, she stamped her feet, put her hands on her hip, threw out her chin, and told me I was stupid beyond belief.

For that reason, I wasn't surprised when Sara said that if I wouldn't tickle the old lady, she wouldn't go to the swamp to catch frogs. We settled into wicker chairs on the shade of the porch and read comic books. The summer sun seared the grass; I could smell the tar melting on the road. At mid-morning, Aunt Flo brought us a picnic basket filled with peanut butter sandwiches and a thermos of fruit juice. She also gave us a dime to buy two frozen Milky Ways and said she would pick us up at three. We pulled shirts over our bathing suits and started the two-mile hike to the village beach.

Two routes led to the bay. We chose the most direct that passed through the dismal swamp. We picked our way along the spongy bank, ignoring the splash of a leaping frog, balancing ourselves on fallen tree trunks that bridged stagnant pools. Reaching the railroad tracks, we climbed the steep embankment and looked both ways. No sign of an approaching train—only the intense heat rising in visible radiant waves from the timber ties and iron rails. The swamp flowed under the embankment through a culvert, a Great Divide. On one side, behind us now, lay the brackish bog; on the other side, still ahead, a string of clear and glistening ponds.

We paused where the water gushed out of the culvert into the small, uppermost lake. I could see orange carp swimming against the current, and in the deeper, more tranquil waters the shadowy bass. We walked on the soft grass (for, despite Aunt Flo's stern warning, we had already removed our shoes) beside the meandering country lane, our bare feet sinking into the fresh-mown turf. On either side there rose large clapboard, brick and stucco houses painted mostly pink or white. I could feel the envy in my bones as we passed the homes of the very rich that looked out over manicured lawns to the shimmering lakes.

We paused again under a weeping willow for a sip of juice. Nearby the water cascaded over a man-made stone dam into the lower and largest of the ponds. In the heart-center of that bottom lake, two aloof white swans glided across the glassy surface. Nearby a family of mallards paddled toward us, mistakenly thinking we would toss them scraps of bread. Farther up the shady shore, several large white domesticated ducks—obviously escapees from some farm—slept with their heads tucked neatly into their tail feathers.

At length we came to the second Great Divide, where the lake water rushed through another culvert under the Montauk Highway. Across the highway the village had built a gazebo where we paused once again and rested on a park bench. I looked to the north and saw the string of freshwater ponds; I turned to the south and saw the mile-long saltwater canal, bulwarked along its banks, with pleasure boats moored on either side.

All at once I realized that in our short walk we had passed through several worlds. Somewhere, probably not far from our house, underground springs bubbled up to form the swamp inhabited by frogs. The swamp drained into the freshwater ponds, and the ponds flowed into the saltwater creek, which emptied into the bay. And out there, beyond my vision, I pictured the bay funneling through narrow inlets into the sea.

But it was the boat-lined canal, arrow straight, that intrigued me now. Sara and I strolled on the narrow strip of grass between the road and the bulkheading, rattling off the names of the vessels as we passed by: *Shindig, Nimrod, Windigo, Mary P., Teeter-Totter, Seven Seas, Northern Star.* Some were posh cabin cruisers with carpeted floors and portholes shaded by venetian blinds; others were spare fishing skiffs with flying bridges and long outrigger rods. There was a tubby yawl with flying pennants and a commodious cockpit; and there was a stripped-down racing sloop with two holes at mid-deck, each barely large enough to contain a squatting skipper and his crew. There were twin-powered yachts that left deep wakes astern as they plowed out of the basin; and stubby, converted clamboats that chugged noisily up the creek. There was even a gaudily painted Chinese junk,

17

which seemed to be there solely for its decorative value, for I never once saw it leave its berth.

Through that summer, Sara and I ambled past these boats on many a summer day, and by the time school opened in September the names affixed to their transoms were firmly impressed in our minds. Sara had a favorite —a gleaming cabin cruiser with a varnished hull owned by two rich, masculine widows whom we often saw scurrying about the deck, barking orders at a youth not much older than myself who helped them haul in lines. I saw him often, his skin bronze from the sun, and wondered how he learned enough about the ways of boats to qualify for such a job. But, unlike Sara, I liked all the boats —or perhaps I didn't have a favorite because I hadn't yet seen the one I wanted to call my own.

Sometimes we would wander out along the bulkheaded breakwaters that jutted toward the center of the canal at right angles to the shore. On one breakwater we invariably found the same solitary snapper fisherman with a long bamboo pole. An elderly man, he sat in a folding chair, dozing in the sun, but whenever he saw us he suddenly came alive and told us which boats had already gone in and out that day. "*Neptune* has already been out and back with the gulls following her wake," he would say, "but you should've been here yesterday afternoon. *Windigo* came barreling down the creek with her spinnaker flying off her bow. Yes sir, that was something to see."

I doubt if I could have made the long trek in such good spirits if I weren't diverted by such information. I had no idea what a spinnaker was, but the mere word conjured up a vivid image. I pictured *Windigo* slicing silently

18

through the water, powered only by an invisible wind that billowed in her sails.

By the time we reached the beach, we were sticky with sweat. We peeled off our clothes, dropped them in the burning sand and plunged into the cool waters of the bay. The first few feet, where the gentle surf deposited stones and shells, were coarse but once the swimmer passed that point the bottom was sandy and firm. I found I could swim for long distances underwater by digging my hands into the bay bottom and pulling myself ahead. The water was pure and clear and I could see objects distinctly. I saw Sara's legs and swam between them, hoisting her willowy body on my shoulders. Even though she was older, I was already stronger and bigger and had no trouble dunking her at will.

Afterwards, we sat on our towels and ate our lunch. It was a dry and cloudless day with little vapor in the air to impair the vision. I glanced across the bay at the distant lighthouse on Fire Island, which seemed near enough to touch. I could see the shiny water towers at Saltaire and Ocean Beach, and stretched between them I could make out the trace of summer homes. The houses seemed to be floating on air, as if they were standing on stilts or had magically suspended themselves above the ground. I yearned to comb the barrier beach, but I knew there was no way to reach that faraway spit of land except by boat.

Then the wind, so still before, picked up—a thin breeze that raised cool prickles on the flesh. It seemed to rise amid the white bleached dunes of Fire Island and gather strength as it crossed the open bay. It was a persistent wind that drove before it the taste of land, leaving only the scent of reeds and razor clams and brine. I detected the breeze first as ripples on the placid surface, then as small, choppy waves that lapped the beach. Within a half-hour the wind had come up briskly, blowing steadily out of the southwest, flashing whitecaps everywhere.

A small sloop skimmed across the beach, not a hundred yards offshore. All at once it changed its course, and then, just as unexpectedly, changed course a second time. It had come from nowhere like a delicate sea bird that dipped and hovered and soared. It was sailed by two boys who seemed, like the sloop itself, to be immersed in the wind and waves.

A moment later I saw a second sloop, and then a third. I walked to the water's edge and stood ankle deep, watching the gathering of sails. Now I counted ten or more spirited sloops, flitting in the spanking breeze. I realized that the long canal we had passed was only one of many natural creeks, and now the sloops—as though awakened by the wind—were sweeping to sea out of these waterways.

I was no longer a bystander on the beach. I was aboard the sloop, leaning to windward, feeling the spray. I marveled at the way the boats angled into the waves, toward that point on Fire Island where I supposed the wind began. There was a mystery I knew I would never solve by standing on the shore.

I sensed someone beside me. I turned and Sara touched my hand. "Would you like a sailboat, Rick?" she said. "I will get Daddy to buy us a sailboat. Just you wait and see."

2 ⁓

It was quite possible to manipulate Uncle Bert; I was sure Sara could manage that with no trouble at all. She played on her mother's anxiety and her father's generosity with virtuosic skill.

Whenever Sara desired something new, she would start on Aunt Flo, who would tell her she was a selfish child who never appreciated what she already had. Aunt Flo was forever telling Sara to "Waste not, want not!" and reminding me that "Children were starving in Greece" whenever I refused to eat the cauliflower I abhorred.

Once Aunt Flo was properly riled up, Sara would work on her father who would say, "I don't know, sweetheart, we'll have to see." Uncle Bert always responded in that indefinite way, for he was incapable of coming right out with an emphatic "No!" He couldn't deny his daughter—or, for that matter, anyone else—anything he felt might be within his power to provide.

When Aunt Flo found out that Uncle Bert was actually considering one of Sara's requests, she would either succumb to a migraine headache or else go into a three-day housecleaning binge. Eventually the matter would erupt into an ugly argument about money when it really didn't concern money at all. It was really about Sara. They were constantly vying with each other over who was going to buy her love.

Uncle Bert would always lose. He would retreat and Aunt Flo would savor her triumph for a few days while Sara pouted, refused to eat, and pretended she was too sick to get up for school. Then Aunt Flo, who had conquered her husband, would concede to her daughter. She would relent and start to make "sacrifices" so they could scrape together the money to buy Sara the one possession that would bring her happiness.

Of course, once Sara obtained what she wanted she would immediately decide she really wanted something else, and round and round they'd go.

I avoided these skirmishes as best I could by keeping my distance and laying my private plans. I saw fairly early that it was one thing to manipulate Uncle Bert and quite another to learn how to sail. It seemed to me that if I first acquired the skill of sailing, then the sailboat would follow naturally. This idea became an article of faith that sustained me. I didn't know how it would happen, but I was sure that if I could only learn to sail then I would own a sloop of my own someday.

There were times when the situation seemed altogether hopeless. Yet for two years I nurtured that dream. I went to the local library and brought home "how-to" books about sailing, but they were worthless as far as I was concerned. I couldn't concentrate on the diagrams or make sense of the nautical terms. When I started to

read a technical description about "the science of tacking" I saw those delicate, white-sailed sloops dipping and
soaring like terns.

When I entered Junior High, my chance came—or so
I thought. I was assigned a seat in English beside Jack
Slatterly, who was known as the best young Snipe skipper on the bay. I was informed that he had already won
a case full of trophies in his Snipe, a 16-foot racing sloop
which was the most popular class for young sailors at
that time. There was no doubt that I was a better English
student than Slatterly, but I felt Slatterly was my superior by far because he knew how to sail. All I had to do
was befriend Slatterly and he would pass on the lore of
sailing and possibly even ask me to be his crew.

But Slats wasn't about to disclose the acquired knowledge that set him apart. Whenever I asked him a question
about sailing, he would shrug his shoulders and walk
away, as if it were beneath his dignity to answer such
questions. A lanky youth, he would stroll through the
school corridors with the air of one who knows a pro-
found secret that he isn't about to share. "I, Slats Slatterly," he seemed to say, "will not discuss sailing with
those unfortunate underlings who aren't already versed
in the art."

I persisted anyhow, mainly because I felt I had nothing to lose. I avoided the direct query as much as possible. Rather than asking a specific question, I would try
to steer the conversation toward sailing in general in the
hope that Slats would drop a morsel of information without meaning to.

One warm spring day I was sitting with a group of
boys on the school lawn. We weren't supposed to be

there, but in those days Bay Shore Junior and Senior High combined numbered barely four hundred students, and so the rules were quite lax. Ward McLaughlin, the school principal, didn't seem to mind our sitting on the front lawn during a study period; he was a wise and kindly man who recognized the folly of trying to coop up boys and girls in a classroom when the dogwood was in bloom.

While I sat there, half listening to the conversation, I could feel—as I so often did—the wind from the bay that wafted over the land. Even though I couldn't sail, I was already conscious of the fact that there wasn't one wind, but many winds, and each had its own distinct character. The wind rarely blew, I noticed, directly from the north or south, but invariably from the compass quadrants, the northeast or southwest. No two winds were the same.

The northeast wind was usually light and puffy and the northwest wind a howling winter gale. The southeast wind was by far the wettest, and it could kick up furiously for days on end. But the prevailing summer wind was like clockwork from the southwest, rising all day and falling all night; and that was the wind, absent all winter, that I felt that spring day in my bones.

During a lull in the conversation, I casually observed that now spring had arrived Slats was probably thinking about putting his boat back in the water. It was a major gaffe. How could I possibly know that winning skippers like Slats hauled their boats after every race so they wouldn't become water-logged? The lighter the boat, the faster she sailed. Slats, glancing at the sky, said that he had never heard a more preposterous remark. I wanted to disappear, but I was rescued by Neil Oden who said,

"Hey Rick, if you want to sail so much, why don't you come out with me?"

That brought a smirk from Slats. "What are you talking about, Oden?" he said. "You don't even own a boat!"

"Oh yes I do," Neil said.

I had mixed feelings about Neil. He was always offering himself as the final authority on any subject, which is the best way of being ignored. But being ignored was the one thing Neil couldn't abide. He longed for friendship but had no idea how to make friends. Whenever a group of boys gathered, he would stand on the fringe and laugh at the most ridiculous comment. The whole time he was really waiting for a chance to express an opinion that he hoped would lead to acceptance, but which never did.

And yet I felt sorry for him too. It was painful, this separation. Like me, Neil belonged to no clique—although I deliberately kept myself aloof. I wasn't going to let anyone get too close. I might approach others for information, but never for warmth, friendship or love. And now Neil Oden was reaching out to me. "All right, Oden," I thought to myself, "go ahead and reach out. You've got a sailboat, and that's one thing in your favor for now."

As it turned out, the boat Neil said he owned belonged to his twenty-three-year-old brother. Neil didn't ask his brother's permission to use the boat; he sneaked the sail-bag out of the house and together we lugged it down to the long canal. It wasn't much of a boat at that. It was a 12-foot dinghy with a stick stuck near the bow for a mast. When we stepped aboard I discovered it had about as much stability as an overloaded canoe. If we both

25

moved suddenly to the same side we'd capsize. Since neither of us had an abundance of boat-sense, we nearly tipped over several times just trying to hoist the sail.

It was a fair wind, a sprightly Memorial Day breeze fresh out of the southwest. It was everything I had hoped for in a wind, and the only difficulty was that neither of us knew how to employ it to advantage. As we pushed off the mooring post, the boat slipped sideways across the narrow canal. "Drop the centerboard, you jerk!" Neil screamed at me. "If you know so much," I shouted back, "drop the centerboard yourself!" The gunwale slammed against the pier and the flimsy boom swung out over the land. While I fended off, Neil figured out how to drop the centerboard and trim the sail. We pushed off again. Now, at least, we were going forward instead of sideways.

But there was another problem. The wind was blowing right into our faces as we sailed out. We had to tack, but we never seemed to gather enough momentum to bring the bow across the wind. Neil was furiously shouting directions at me while I tended the main sheet, which was already tangled with all sorts of other lines. Meanwhile, the sloop kept heading up to the wind, luffing momentarily, and slipping back on the same tack. I didn't know why it was happening; all I knew was that Neil kept telling me it was all my fault.

"It's back-winding," he kept shouting. "Can't you see it's back-winding!"

I'd have done anything to keep the mainsail from "back-winding," but I didn't know what the term meant. And I suspected Neil didn't either.

We collided with most of the boats moored in the canal

as we aimed for the bay. Then we were free and clear at last. Neil sailed on a broad reach. The wind came over my shoulder as I leaned to windward to keep us upright. I felt the relentless tug of the wind as I seized the main sheet, not knowing enough to give it a turn around a cleat to ease the strain. My palm was rubbed raw, but I didn't realize it. All I knew was that I was sailing, sailing at last. The boat was heeling and the water was rushing past and Neil was positively white with fright.

Then, behind us, I saw another sloop bearing down like a mightly galleon.

"He wants to race!" I shouted at Neil. "Look at that! He wants to race!"

It was a foolhardy notion to think that the first time out in a sailboat I could compete with a sloop twice as large. I trimmed the mainsheet and our dinghy heeled over even further, but still the other boat gained.

As the sloop came up to windward I could see it was the *Juno,* a 26-foot Zephyr owned by Susan Johns. I saw her sitting in the cockpit, her blond hair blowing in the wind, an amused expression on her face, as if she knew something I had yet to learn. Then I saw the skipper was Slats. I waved my free hand, but he was bent on passing as close as possible without acknowledging our existence. He swept up on our windward and without ado stole the wind from our sails.

Blanketed by *Juno*'s enormous mainsail, our tiny sail collapsed. It luffed, flat and empty, and the boom swung crazily, which would have been all right if Neil and I had anticipated it. Afraid we were going to come about, we both lurched to the opposite side of the boat at the same time, and as the sail filled again with wind the dinghy

27

tipped over, spilling us both into the bay.

Hanging on with one hand to the bow of the capsized boat, I raised my other in a clenched fist of defiance at Slats and Sue, who didn't even have enough interest to turn around and witness the havoc they had caused. I was overcome at first with righteous indignation and then I was filled with awe. I saw Slats lean forward and haul in the main sheet, hand over hand. As he did so, *Juno*'s mainsail bellied more fully and the sloop swung higher into the wind. It was an eloquent motion, full of silent force and grace. Somewhere Neil was hollering at me to stand on the exposed centerboard and help right the capsized boat, but I was only aware of the swerving beauty of *Juno* as she sailed away.

Neil and I sailed together many times that summer in his brother's dinghy, and the outcome was always the same. No matter how often we tacked out the narrow canal, we always slammed into the bulkhead, slipping sideways faster than we surged ahead. We rarely built sufficient speed to bring the light bow of the boat across the face of the wind. The principles of momentum eluded Neil, mainly because he had no innate sense of the velocity or direction of the breeze. He failed to grasp the essential fact that the boat itself is a weathervane.

"Fend off! Fend off!" he would shout and send me scampering from side to side. I felt he was more interested in ordering me about than making maximum use of the spanking breeze. When at last we reached open water, Neil would bark, "Ready about! Hard-a-lee," as if he were the sharp-tongued captain of a brigantine. Then he would repeat his stunt of bringing the boat into the wind and falling back on the same tack again. By the end of the summer he had mastered all the nautical terms and commands; he knew everything about a sailboat except how to sail.

Whenever we capsized, he would blame the mishap either on the elements or his crew. "Did you see that puff?" he would say when the wind was steady from the west. "It came out of nowhere!" Or else he would sputter after a dunking, "I told you to hike to windward, didn't I?" In truth, some of the fault may have been mine. I handled the main sheet and there were times, I'm sure, when I failed to trim it properly or let it run out fast enough through my burning hands. But I also found it impossible to foresee what Neil would do.

He never let me take the tiller; he always steered himself, seizing the stick tightly and yanking it to and fro, stiff-armed, as if the boat were propelled not by the wind but by the mechanical force he imparted to the rudder. The net result was loss of forward thrust—or an accidental jibe that flipped us overboard. One day while we were bailing out the cockpit I said, "Neil, why don't you let me take the tiller for a change."

"Not now," he said. "The wind is too tricky for you today."

"Oden," I said, reaching for the most demeaning epithet one sailor could call another on the Great South Bay, "you're a plumber. You couldn't sail a soap dish in a bath tub."

He looked at me, stung, as if I had abused his friendship in some way. But I didn't care; I ached for the feel of the tiller and knew I didn't stand a chance of touching it as long as I sailed with Neil.

I vowed I'd never sail with him again. When we reached shore, I walked off, leaving him to clean up and lug the sailbag home alone. But the next day he called me as if nothing had happened and once again we tacked out of the narrow canal, repeating the mistakes of the day before.

It was the fourth day of a brisk southwester that blew straight into our teeth. The water was roughest near the mouth of the canal where the bay chop struck the concrete wharf of a whitewashed beach club. A half dozen members hung over a railing, watching the boats maneuver in and out of the canal, and occasionally they were treated to a thrill, like a dinghy tipping over before their eyes. Whenever that happened, they would let out a cheer—to the mortification of the sailors floundering in the sea.

As usual, Neil failed to maintain sufficient momentum, and soon the boat was being buffeted on one side by the waves plowing across the bay and on the other by the backwash off the wharf. It was obvious that if we didn't come about soon we would be dashed against the wall. It was the moment I had been waiting for. Neil turned to me in desperation. "Take the tiller," he said. "Bring her about! See what you can do."

We switched places. "Trim the sail as tight as you can," I said, and headed slightly off the wind. As she gained headway, I held her there, and then with no warning (for I was sick of Neil's infuriating commands) I shoved the tiller as hard as I could toward the sail. The frail bow crossed the breeze with barely a luff and we were instantly off on a broad reach with the sail close-hauled. We were knocked down in that dangerous moment when the hull sits nearly still in the water and the sail suddenly fills on the opposite side. The sea rushed over the coaming into the cockpit. The dinghy valiantly tried to right herself, like a stricken sea bird, but the saturated sail was too heavy a counterweight to our hiking bodies and she rolled over on her side.

"You plumber, you stupid plumber," Neil shouted as we swam around the partially submerged boat.

"What do you mean—plumber?" I said. "I brought her about, didn't I!"

We beached the boat off the private club and I relived my mistake, born of desperation and inexperience. It struck me that the skill of tacking lay somewhere between Neil's hesitant maneuvers and my bold ones. There was more delicacy to sailing than I had dreamed.

Sara had moved into the front bedroom, vacated by Grandma Bessie who languished in a nursing home, while I occupied a back bedroom barely larger than a pantry, which appeared to have been built as an afterthought between the kitchen and the porch. It was a stuffy place in summer, poorly ventilated; in winter it was frigid, the last room to receive heat from a furnace fueled with coal. But it wasn't the size of the bedroom that bothered me as much as its proximity to the kitchen where Sara and Aunt Flo clashed. At those moments I wished we lived in a mansion with a maze of halls that led to a vaulted retreat known to me alone.

Those tempests had at least one saving grace: they gathered force slowly if ineluctably—I could see them brewing a long way off. The first warning signal was a lament from Sara about some possession she lacked and needed at once if she were to survive another day on earth. Aunt Flo would respond by rattling her pots and pans as if her daughter didn't exist. But Sara had already told me how she could gauge the level of her mother's anxiety by the way she blinked her eyes and twitched her head. As Aunt Flo's tic intensified, Sara would escalate her attack. When Aunt Flo couldn't stand it anymore, she would blurt out, "Sara, you're a selfish, ungrateful child!" With that, Sara would withdraw and sulk over the injustice of her mother's stern rebuke. After all, she was only asking for a fourposter with a canopy over the top, like the one her best friend Isabel had. The thought of Isabel sleeping in such a lovely bed preyed on Sara's mind, and soon enough she was back again, strumming on her mother's nerves. Aunt Flo contained her emotions, smiling blandly, twitching her head; but the pressure built within her pain-wracked body and she erupted with volcanic force.

Of course, there were intervals of tranquility too. Hostilities always ceased whenever Aunt Flo gathered us around the radio to listen to her favorite saga, *One Man's Family*. The progenitor of the family in this soap opera bore the surname of Barber, and he and his self-effacing wife lived in splendid isolation on an estate along the Pacific Coast where the ocean pounded futilely against a sturdy sea wall. Periodically, one or another of the Barber offspring, now married, would return to the family residence, bringing their spouses and their woes. They never called the elderly pair Mom and Pop, but always Mother and Father or, better yet, Mother Barber and Father Barber. As Aunt Flo listened to the travails of the Barber clan, the tension flowed from her face. She was no longer a beleaguered housewife trapped in a nuclear family where nerves rubbed raw; she was a matriarch surrounded by adoring children in a Great House eternally protected from the onslaught of the sea.

Our tiny bungalow was far more vulnerable. One winter morning a howling wind woke me at dawn. I snuggled under the covers, burying my head for warmth. I rolled over on my stomach, then, poking my head out like a turtle, gazed through the window behind my bed at the white quilt across the yard. During the night the snow had fallen, melted on the trees, then frozen, encasing the twigs in a glistening glass. Behind the porch, a symmetrical white oak had been spreading its branches for nearly a century; in summer it was a glorious shade tree, but now in the dead of winter it was standing rigidly against a northwest gale. Suddenly I heard a crack, sharp as a shot, and the roof crunched like cardboard overhead. One overhanging branch, stiff with cold and age, had parted at the trunk and landed on the ell that was my room. A cracked rafter poked through the ceiling and plaster dust floated in the air and settled in my hair. I lay stockstill, afraid that if I moved the walls would come tumbling down about my bed. Finally I heard Uncle Bert calling me from the kitchen and I picked my way, shivering and barefoot, over the debris.

Oddly enough, Aunt Flo could accept such natural disasters with equanimity. "It was an act of God," she explained, and that made it bearable for her. She could endure bolts from above; it was the acts of the mortals around her that drove her to distraction. Uncle Bert surveyed the damage and sucked in his cheeks. He knew acts of God could be costly, but he didn't know this one would change our lives.

When the wind stopped, a builder came and patched the hole in the ceiling. Then he returned later in the week to repair the roof. Each evening he would stop by the bungalow and talk over the construction details with Uncle Bert. The job wasn't all that complicated, and after a while their conversation veered toward other subjects. The two men were drawn to each other, for they had those complementery traits that so often form the basis of a lasting friendship. Uncle Bert had a strong sense of finance; he knew all about such abstruse matters as deeds, titles and mortgages, but he couldn't drive a nail without bending it. The builder, whose name was Ed Doubrava, was oblivious to money mainly because he didn't need it. When he wanted something he built it, and what he couldn't fashion with his hands he didn't want.

I was taken by this man, so different from any other I had ever known. He asked me to hoist two-by-fours to where he was working amid the rafters, and he even let me saw one, showing me how to start the blade so that it cut evenly along a line. He also asked me what I liked to do. When I said I liked to sail, he told me how the Great South Bay froze over from shore to shore when he was a boy, and how he had built an ice boat for himself and skimmed across the slick surface quicker than the wind. But now he liked to cruise the bay in a 30-foot power boat that he moored behind his house in one of those winding creeks that fed into the bay. He said that sometimes he built summer homes on Fire Island and

34

that when I was older and needed a job he would hire me. I thought about his power boat and tried to envision what sort of lines she had. I wondered how much accumulated lore about the bay—its secret passages and hidden harbors—was stored in Ed Doubrava's head.

One evening Uncle Bert, Aunt Flo and Ed Doubrava chatted in the living room well past bedtime. Sara and I eavesdropped from the kitchen, pretending we were amusing ourselves with an endless game of Monopoly, which we always played. Uncle Bert said he had his eye on a piece of property closer to the bay on a street that ran parallel to the long canal. He wanted to build a house on that site, which he would subsequently sell. "I think the market is right," he said, "for the kind of house I have in mind." He talked about what the house would look like: how many bathrooms and bedrooms it would have. It was a two-story house, a modified Cape with a dormer shed across the back. He warmed to his subject and the house came alive.

While my bedroom was being rebuilt, my bed was moved into Sara's room. We lay in our separate beds, surrounded by darkness, sharing our secret thoughts. We talked about the prospect of a new house being built so close to the water, and we imagined the vast sums of money Uncle Bert would realize from the sale. Although I didn't say so, I thought perhaps he might make enough to buy a small sailboat for me. Then another notion crossed my mind.

"It's too bad," I said, "that the house won't be ours when it's finished."

"But don't you see," Sara said, "it will be ours. That's the point of it. The house will be ours."

"But Sara," I said, "your father distinctly said he intends to sell it. Didn't you hear him? He said he can't make any money unless he sells it."

"Poor Rick," Sara said, "you don't understand at all. Daddy says he will sell the house because that's the only way Mommy will let him build it. But after it's built, she'll decide that we'll have to make a giant sacrifice and move into it ourselves because this bungalow is just too small."

I lay awake for a long time, thinking about what Sara had said. The way of the world seemed terribly roundabout to me. Uncle Bert was deceiving Aunt Flo, and Aunt Flo was deceiving herself, but in the end we would all move into the new Cape, which was exactly what everyone wanted anyhow.

I listened to the voices in the other room, the width of a wall away. Sometimes they were muffled, but occasionally they rose in laughter and excitement. Doubrava was a catalyst, inducing confidence and calm. Even Aunt Flo sounded content, going along, not anticipating obstacles that would never arise. For the first time since my parents died, I felt warm, as if I belonged, had a home. But the mood was ephemeral; it evaporated with the night and by the next morning my wintry isolation had returned.

The thaw came early that year. By mid-April the land was cleared and the concrete cellar had cured in the ground. By the time the dogwood bloomed Ed Doubrava and two carpenters had framed the house. Every day after school Sara and I wandered through the wooden skeleton, squeezing between studs, pretending the rooms were already furnished and occupied. Sara staked her claim to a large upstairs bedroom with windows on two walls that faced north and west. We still had no assurance that this house would be ours, but that didn't deter her from marching through the rooms with the pride of ownershop.

"Yes, Sara," I said, "that will be a lovely room for you." By then she had acquired her fourposter and was trying to figure out which wall it should go against. But I was thinking how the bitter winds of February came from the north and west, rattling the panes and whistling through the sills. It would be far more suitable, I thought, to have a small room with a single window that faced south and trapped the balmy summer breeze from the bay.

"And which room would you like, Rick?" she asked. Since there were only two bedrooms left, and one was a master bedroom, she hadn't left me much choice. The one destined for me seemed to be downstairs, abutting the kitchen again. But I shrugged in response, as if I hadn't noticed the way she narrowed my options. I couldn't picture what the interior would look like once the walls were up, but I was hoping a hermitage would materialize for me somewhere under the eaves far away from heavy traffic.

One day Ed (who insisted that Sara and I call him this and not Mr. Doubrava, though it took a while to get used to) beckoned me to where he was standing between two sawhorses, a hammer in one hand and a broom in the other. "Rick," he said, "how would you like to earn three bucks a week?" My eyes widened. When I first arrived at the Mann house, Uncle Bert would give Sara and me a quarter every Saturday morning. "Here's twenty-five cents for you," he would say to Sara, "and twenty-five cents for you," he would say to me. It was an accounting ritual, I soon realized, that had very little to do with the disbursement of funds. What Uncle Bert was actually saying was: "What I give to one I also give to the other." Later he raised our weekly allowance to fifty cents and then to a dollar, but he always doled it out openly, first to Sara and then to me, but with the disinterest of a judge.

Now I was being offered three dollars a week to perform tasks I probably would have done for nothing. I could start a boat fund and save to buy a dinghy like the one Neil's brother owned. I hadn't yet learned how easy it is to spend small sums on temptations nearer at hand.

"I sure would," I replied.

"All right," he said, and handed me the broom and set me to work sweeping sawdust and woodchips. I was a methodical worker, going from room to room with broom and dust pan, heaping trash in an oil drum outside. Occasionally Ed let me saw a stud or pound a nail, but not until he explained the function of a particular board or brace. I loved the aroma of fresh-sawn wood; at night I dreamed of joists and rafters joined to form a huge gabled roof.

Then one Saturday morning Ed showed me how to put up sheathing for the outside wall. I sheathed the back porch and the rear of the attached garage. I had always felt I wasn't handy, but Ed dispelled whatever qualms I had. "Here," he said, "I want you to put up this sheathing. There's nothing to it. I'll show you how." The tongued boards fit together, one above the other, like roughhewn flooring laid on its side. Each time I nailed another board I felt as though I had personally given the house additional form and solidity.

Years later, when I hired a contractor to build a house for my family, I remembered how I once helped sheathe the Mann house, which stands to this day. I also discovered to my sorrow that in an age of plywood sheets they don't make houses the way they used to. The builder assured me that his plywood was as strong as my sheathing, but I was skeptical, and still am.

While I worked, Sara wandered aimlessly about the site as though I had deserted her. She was now 15, an age when a girl might find a brother two years younger an encumbrance. But I wasn't her brother and that made all the difference. Since we hadn't grown up together, we didn't take each other for granted the way ordinary siblings do. We were both only children tossed together by fate, but I don't think I was ever as lonely as she.

"What do you want to do that for?" she asked, taunting me as I gave a nailhead a final rap and then stepped back to admire my workmanship. For every minute I spent working I spent two admiring.

"Don't talk to me," I said. "Can't you see I'm busy now?"

"If my mother finds out you're building this house instead of Ed she won't care for it at all."

"Your mother won't find out—unless you tell her."

"I just might. She hired Ed to build this house, not you."

"I'm not building this house. I'm just sheathing the porch and the garage."

"That's part of the house, isn't it? I wouldn't be surprised if the whole back end blew away because of you."

"Sara, the back end isn't going to blow away because of me."

"One good hurricane," she persisted, "and the entire back end will blow away."

"Sara," I said, "why don't you ride your bike down to the village and buy each of us an ice cream sandwich. I have lots of money now." She had a new bike with thin racing tires and when she wasn't looking I would steal a ride. Her bike was much easier to pedal than my antique model with thick balloon tires that my parents had bought for me years before.

"Why don't you go yourself?" she said.

"Because I'm working. Can't you see!"

I held out some loose change in my palm, which she studied, making sure I had enough. She reached out to knock the coins to the ground, but I anticipated her intent and pulled my hand away in time.

"Sara," I said, "what ails you anyhow?"

She glared at me, hands on her hips, eyes ablaze, consumed by a jealousy I didn't understand. Then she softened, took the money and sped off to the store. I watched her as she disappeared, wondering what I possessed that she could possibly want. Her dark moods seemed to rise without warning. When she returned we lay back against a mound of excavated dirt, a barrier that hid us from the road. I prayed that Aunt Flo wouldn't drive by, for I knew she would be beside herself if she caught us eating ice cream sandwiches so close to supper time.

"What do you think of Ed?" Sara suddenly asked me.

40

"Oh, he's all right, I suppose," I answered as cooly as I could.

"If he were an army captain," she said, "I bet his men would worship him." She was referring to the war, which was a distant rumble on a foreign shore. Young men barely out of high school, young men whose brothers and sisters we knew, had not yet begun to die. The house and the bay and the boats were in the forefront of my consciousness but the blitzkreig was something we'd heard about on the radio. I didn't know if Sara was more aware of the war than I, but she obviously saw Ed Doubrava dashing heroically about the field of battle. "If soldiers had someone like Ed to lead them, they would follow him anywhere, wouldn't they?"

"How should I know?" I said, licking my sticky fingers, picking up my hammer and returning to my job.

Sara always carried a book with her to the building site. While I worked she sat on a pile of lumber or a tree stump, but I noticed she rarely progressed more than a page or two during the course of an afternoon. At first I attributed her inability to concentrate to the excitement of the house coming together before her eyes. I supposed that, like me, she awoke each morning and immediately thought about some aspect of the work that would be finished by quitting time.

Although my father was an artist, I hadn't inherited an essential element of his artistry. For me, a blank canvas was forever blank until he painted a picture there. And so it was with carpentry; I couldn't visualize a house with a shingled roof until the last nail was in place. Each new timber, board and nail altered its character. For that

41

reason I never tired of walking around and through the house, watching it grow and change.

But Sara seemed to divine what the house would look like down to the last detail even before the boards were sawn and nailed. It wasn't the building but the builder that caught her eye. The book was a facade. She held it in front of her face, then gazed over the top while Ed straddled a beam, walked a precarious second-story plank, or twisted his body around a post to clobber a nail. If he looked up her eyes dropped back to the printed page, and I could feel her burning resentment whenever he spoke to me.

He was an easy man to watch, for he moved with fluency despite a physical handicap, the aftermath of a childhood disease. While he was still a boy, he was stricken with polio that affected the left side of his body, especially his arm. His left hand reached only as far as his waist, but the arm itself was fully developed from manual work and its muscles bulged. When I first met him his shortened arm was his most apparent physical characteristic, but now that I knew him better I hardly noticed it at all. That was because he told me it was an asset to have two arms of different length.

"A long arm is good for distance work, like sawing," he said, "while a short arm is good for close-up work, like measuring."

I knew there was an architect somewhere behind the scenes, but Ed never allowed him to show his face or his blueprints on the premises. He had little use for plans, and he proceeded more by instinct than design. A house, to him, was a living organism that grew of its own volition in unexpected ways.

42

One Saturday morning Uncle Bert, Sara and I drove over to the new house. When we arrived, Ed was on the second floor, and he called down the stairwell, "Bert, come up here! I want to show you something."

We climbed the stairs and found him squatting under the rafters, rubbing his chin. At such times I felt he wasn't trying so much to solve a problem as he was waiting for the solution to present itself to his mind. What he had found out was that there was enough space to squeeze another bedroom on the second floor. It would be an L-shaped room that ran parallel to the front of the house and then took a sharp right-angle turn. "We'll have to add a small dormer in the front," he said, "but that won't be too much of a job." He seemed pleased with himself, like an explorer who has stumbled on uncharted land.

"But we already have a third bedroom downstairs," Sara said. "Why should we need another one up here?" I could have throttled her.

Uncle Bert thrust his hands in his pockets and looked at me. "What do you think, Rick," he said. "If this were your house, and you had a choice, where would you rather have your bedroom—upstairs in an L-shaped room or downstairs behind the kitchen?"

I furrowed my brow as if I were giving the problem the courtesy of due thought and then said: "Upstairs." It was the thing I loved about Uncle Bert; he could be counted on.

Ed's discovery, of course, made the downstairs bedroom superfluous, but the completed house had very little logic anyhow. It had two living rooms (one beside the other), two screened porches (both too small to use for anything but storage), and an unforeseen bedroom (mine) on the second floor under the eaves. When the dormer was complete, I entered it alone late one afternoon. It was half the size of Sara's, a cozy place with a window that caught the prevailing summer breeze. Through the window I could see past the side yard of the house across the street between two black willows that framed a section of the Brightwaters Canal. I could sit there by the hour and watch the boats sail by. It was my private view of the world, provided the room was mine.

Each time a prospective buyer looked at the house, Sara and I entered a period of gloom. But as soon as the prospect said the house wasn't for them, we disguised our delight. In their own way, Aunt Flo and Uncle Bert were playing the same deceptive game with us. Finally Aunt Flo accepted the inevitable and broke the news to us one evening at supper.

"Children," she said, "we're going to have to do without some of our luxuries in the days ahead. The fact is that we can't sell the new house, and so we're going to move into it and sell this one instead."

Sara shot a sidelong look at me at the same instant I glanced at her. We tried to suppress our laughter but we exploded and filled the kitchen with contagious joy.

Sitting in my L-shaped room one morning not long after we moved in, I saw the blue sloop for the first time. I was looking at a two-masted Windigo laid up against one of the piers that jutted toward the center of the canal. She was tied fore and aft, and was prevented from swaying at her berth by spring lines. The blue sloop glided

44

down the saltwater creek past the larger yawl, wind astern, graceful as a swan. Her mainsail swelled in the rising breeze and her boom arched upward and outward over the starboard side. She disappeared for a moment, then reappeared, her bow swinging upwind as the helmsman trimmed her sails. She was poised for an instant, fluttering with her sails flat, and suddenly she heeled as the breeze bellied in her sails once more. She sliced across the canal and back again, laying over on her lines, and then she tacked beyond my vision toward the bay. I contrasted the way Neil and I floundered about with the crisp headway of this boat as she crisscrossed the canal. Was it the balance of the sloop or the skill of the helmsman, or a combination of the two? It seemed to me that man and boat were acting in concert to make the most of a flukey breeze that warped around houses and trees lining the shore. There were times when the sloop came so close to the bulkhead I thought she would crash, but always at the precise moment the skipper deftly swung her bow across the wind and angled for the opposite shore. In his unerring judgment, he was using every inch of the narrow waterway. She was gone now, but her blue hull and thrusting bow, her bright decks glistening in the morning sun, were firmly fixed in my mind's eye for a long time.

3 ～

Ed Doubrava liked to dance.

In those days he shared a house with two high school teachers, Josie and Evelyn Stritch. He was affianced to the older sister, Josie, whom he eventually married, but Evelyn, who was fresh out of teacher's college, followed him about, mewing for attention and cuddling up whenever she could. I suspect Ed secretly enjoyed her constant atttentions, although he never gave her any encouragement as far as I could see. As for Josie, she would either look the other way or smile indulgently, as if to say, "There goes my little sister, Evelyn, trying to wrest my man from me again."

It was precisely the sort of domestic arrangement Aunt Flo and Uncle Bert would never have tolerated in another man. This was about as close to concubinage as they were likely to come. But they both had liberal pretensions that ran counter to their conservative instincts. "How others choose to lead their lives," Aunt Flo would say, "is no concern of ours." Then Uncle Bert would add, "That's right, Flo, that's right!" In Uncle Bert's view there was a clear separation of powers in married life. The husband was in charge of money and the wife of moral judgments.

But for Ed Doubrava, sin was suspended and I think I know why. Through him they experienced adventure without risk. It was a new life for Uncle Bert and Aunt Flo, for now they had an open invitation to sail with Ed every weekend aboard his cabin cruiser. In return, Uncle Bert bought the gas and Aunt Flo brought the food. It was a better than even exchange, for the bay beguiled Uncle Bert who would never buy a boat of his own. He abhorred anything mechanical and he couldn't swim a stroke. He would wade in the shallow water up to his waist and then make a hasty retreat for shore. But what he liked best, after a long week in the city, was a quiet weekend on—not in—the water. He would arrive home Friday night, pale and haggard, and after two days cruising the Great South Bay, he would return to business Monday morning, tanned and relaxed.

Aunt Flo liked the water too, but she made it clear that the main reason she went out on Ed's boat was because it did Uncle Bert so much good.

For those reasons, Aunt Flo and Uncle Bert overlooked what they believed to be the truth: that Ed was having affairs with two women, sisters no less. This conviction was never mentioned, at least not in the presence of the children, but the same notion crossed our minds too. One day Sara said to me, "Rick, do you think he likes both of them?"

I was shocked. It was one thing to secretly entertain such thoughts and another to speak about them openly.

But I had reached an age where it was necessary to sound wise in the ways of the world.

"Of course he does," I said. "What do you think!"

Sara seemed delighted by this confirmation of her deepest suspicions, but I was disappointed in myself for my betrayal. I felt Ed was in love with Josie and he was putting up with Evelyn for Josie's sake—at least until the younger sister found a man of her own. In the absence of hard evidence to the contrary, it's always easy to suspect the worst.

In truth, there was a mitigating circumstance that put a cloak of respectability over the Doubrava-Stritch household. Ed was separated but not yet divorced from his first wife. Her name was never mentioned; she was a ghost, buried in his past. But I knew she had custody of their son, who was a few years older than I. I often thought about that absent son, wondered what he looked like and if he realized what he missed.

There was very little Ed Doubrava couldn't do. He could captain a boat, repair an engine, build a house. He could hit towering fungoes or hook slide into second base, which he taught me to do in the world's largest sand pit, the beach at Fire Island. He could ferret out secret coves and build roaring bonfires of driftwood in the dunes.

And he could dance.

Ed lived in a nondescript ranch house that he kept amending and buttressing, adding rooms here and removing others there. But one room he never altered, and that was the living room with its huge stone fireplace and hard wooden floors. It was a lively gathering place for the two family groups, and on almost any evening Ed would roll back the shag rug, wind up the phonograph and play his favorite record, a song called "Hindustan," a melodic, haunting number by the popular pianist, Frankie Carl. He would seize Josie, lifting her out of her chair, and the two would whirl around the floor, reminding me of my mother and father, although their dancing styles were hardly the same.

My parents were slick ballroom dancers who polished their steps. They could go from rhumba to tango to charleston to fox trot. In a pinch they could even waltz. They danced not so much for themselves as for the admiration of others who would stop, watch and applaud. But Ed danced for himself, for the sheer joy of dancing and not its subtle grace. He knew only one step, and he danced that step regardless of the song, although the song was usually "Hindustan." He had athletic control of his body—of his arms, his legs and his torso—and he spun like a dervish as the music gathered him in its ecstatic force.

Midway through the dance, "Hindustan" would start to groan, and I would dash for the phonograph and wind it up again.

Then Ed would relinquish Josie and seize Evelyn, who would put her arms around his neck and press herself against him, making him drag her around the floor. Then he would take Sara who was lithe and limber and could dance with silken airiness. Sara could dance with any man, making him look better than he really was. But after Sara danced with Ed, she wouldn't dance with me. "You're too oafish! Besides, you have no timing," she would say.

Then Josie would grab me and guide me around the

49

floor, while Ed would try to show me how to move my feet. "You don't need a dance step," he would insist. "Just move your feet to the music. That's the way! That's the way!"

Then Aunt Flo and Uncle Bert, caught up in the easy spirit, would come together in the center of the living room floor. I was astonished at Uncle Bert—how he danced alternately on the heels and balls of his feet, bobbing like a cork with Aunt Flo hanging on to him, looking up and smiling at him all the time. I could see a glimmer of what they were when he courted her years before.

One August night, after some spirited dancing, I went outside to cool off in the night air. Ed's house backed on a saltwater creek, a main thoroughfare for boats between Main Street and the bay. It was hemmed in by three boatyards, one down the creek, one on a small island up the creek and another on the opposite shore. In addition, it was surrounded by ferry slips, points of embarkation for Fire Island beach communities. By day commercial and pleasure boats plied the creek, but now, under the summer stars, there was only the silhouette of the berthed ferries, the carrying notes of a piano from a honky-tonk on the town dock, and the muffled conversation of crabbers with the reflected beams of their flashlights across the water and the occasional splash of their traps.

I walked along the narrow pier, wide enough for one person and quite misshapen, for the ice of many winters had raised the pilings and buckled the planks. I stood alongside *Jove*, Ed's boat (the Jo was for Josie and the Ve for Evelyn). She was 30 feet long from stem to stern and, like everything else Ed owned, more noteworthy for her practicality than her style. Low and beamy with a rakish hull that rose high in the bow, she spoke of seamanship and simple pleasures. She had a long trunk cabin with four comfortable berths plus a galley; her commodious cockpit was covered with a canopy from wheel to transom. If we wanted to sun ourselves we could sit on the cabin, but most of the time we sought protection from the elements. When it rained, Ed stretched a canvas between the canopy and the deck. The protective canvas also served as a windbreaker, and so it was possible to sail *Jove* in comfort on any day when there wasn't a gale or ice.

I climbed aboard and sat on the transom, dangling my legs. A small, flat-bottomed clamboat chugged down the creek; I could hear the separate firings of her pistons and I wondered why she was coming home so late. Then I saw the skipper standing upright in his doghouse, big enough for him alone, while his wife and two small children sat on box crates on the deck. He had taken his family for a pleasant evening cruise, maybe visiting a friend on another creek.

A screen door slammed at the honky-tonk and a heavyset man, his belly bulging under his belt, staggered along the dock. I thought he would pitch overboard headfirst, but he reached slowly down to a cleat and pulled his dory to the wharf. He stepped aboard and stood in the stern, sure-footed as a goat, and sculled his way across the creek with one oar jammed in a lock. I guessed he was one of the charter-boat captains who lived in one of the many small two-story houses with sharply sloping roofs along the shore. I noticed that these men never sat and rowed but always stood and sculled, propelling the boat with fluent motions of the arms and wrist. A spark of envy shot through me. I could row but I couldn't scull, and that set me apart from a world I wanted to join.

"Ah, there you are!" a voice said. It was Ed, who had come outside to check the lines. "I have some news for you."

"Really," I said, feigning nonchalance. "About what?"

"About the leaning house of Oak Island," he said. "It's an old house with a widow's walk and an awkward tilt. We've got to straighten it out."

"Three dollars a day," I said.

"Make it five. You'll earn it. We'll be there several days and will live aboard *Jove.*"

I'd have gone just to be with him. He held out his hand. I grabbed it and leaped from the stern to the dock. As I landed I saw Sara's eyes glowing like a tigress in the dark at the end of the pier.

"Can Sara come too?"

"Of course," he said. "That is, if her mother will let her."

"Why wouldn't my mother let me?" Sara said.

"I'll arrange it," Ed said. He returned to the house, put an old-fashioned waltz on the phonograph and danced Aunt Flo around the room.

Sara and I sat in silence on *Jove*'s stern and watched her wake, white and foaming, as it spread and disappeared. Only a crackling fire can cast the same hypnotic spell. Every now and then I would lift my eyes and look toward land to keep myself from sinking into a trance.

52

Jove didn't have the steep wake of a ferry, the kind that can tip a small boat caught by her swells. And she didn't have the barely visible wake of a sloop that could pass through the water without a trace as a bird through the air. Her wake was surface-deep, bubbling up from her churning prop, raising a gentle wave that might lap for miles until it reached a shore.

The wake of a boat is a measure of her forward thrust, and *Jove* was meant to make way leisurely. On early summer mornings the Great South Bay is often enveloped in a light mist, as it was this day. *Jove* skimmed along the placid surface amid shoal-draft clamboats that seemed to squat on the still water while strong-armed diggers lowered and raised their long rakes and tongs. Gradually the rising sun burned off the mist and the shoreline, green and dense with foliage, emerged—a huge cylindrical gas tank and the lone spire of St. Peter's by the Sea looming over it all.

As the land receded, my nostrils filled with the pungent aroma of the tidal marsh and my head cleared. We were heading for the barren island world where the wind began. When I awoke I had a touch of hayfever, and a sneezing fit warned me that the first traces of ragweed pollen were in the air. I could never understand why something so essential to nature was so alien to my eyes and nose. But the faint wind that picked up now drove landward from the barrier beach and it was filled with brine that cleansed the air.

I left the stern and, seizing a handrail, swung into the cockpit and stood by the wheel. Ed steered for a point west of the Fire Island Light; he said he was watching for a clam bed marker, a stake with many branches that

53

rose from the shoals like a leafless tree. When we sighted it, a half-dozen other similiar markers appeared at the same time. He wound his way around and between those markers, emerging off the easterly tip of Captree Island, so close I could almost reach out and touch the marsh grass that grew along the shore.

"Shortcut," he explained, cutting the engine so that the stern would ride even higher in the water than before. "This close to land there's always two and a half feet of water, even at low tide. Twenty feet further out we would run aground." I memorized the way he threaded the markers and the secret passages across the flats. I studied the channels and shoals, noting not only the changes in the colors but also the variations in the waves.

As we rounded the island I saw a relic, the gutted timber frame of the Wa Wa Yonda Club, a casino during Prohibition Days. Now it was a forlorn and deserted building, buffeted by salt winds, its wharf askew and its boardwalk buried in the bog. Years later it was ravaged by fire and totally disappeared. But now it remained a useful landmark for baymen seeking the state boat channel, which separates Captree Island from Captree Beach. That waterway was marked like a superhighway with black posts bearing white arrows that pointed toward the dredged center, as if wayward boatmen had to be told where the deep water lay. Today a drawbridge passes over that channel, linking Robert Moses Causeway with Robert Moses Bridge, which leads to Robert Moses State Park. But on that day there was no causeway, no drawbridge, no state park—only a handful of boats plying the channel and a great blue heron wading unperturbed along the shore.

Now we were far from the taste of the mainland, where I knew the sun was starting to bake the earth, creating conditions for the onshore breeze. As the warm air rose the cooler air rushed in, sweeping from the ocean across the bay, gaining in strength as the day wore on. But here, separated from the ocean by a spit of sand, the mild seawind caressed my face. I felt as if I had crossed an unmarked boundary and entered the habitat that was my natural home.

The channel widened. Across the water I saw summer homes, perhaps fifty in all. They faced south toward the sea, overlooking another narrow channel that flowed like a private inlet past their front doors. Nearly every house had a rickety dock to which the owner had tied a row-boat, his sole link between the main road that ran along the barrier beach and his island home. The houses were side by side, and while they all seemed to bear a family resemblance, no two were the same. Some were high two-story affairs with widow's walks and some were low one-story affairs with warped decks across the front. Then I realized it was the combination of weather and age that made them all appear as if they were cut from a common mold.

As we approached, Ed told me most of the houses were founded on timber pilings driven as deep as possible into the underlying bog. Sooner or later, he said, they started to sink or sag. It was one of these sagging houses that he had been hired to straighten out, although how one set a leaning house aright was more than I could under-stand. I wondered which house it was, but Ed didn't volunteer that information and I didn't ask. I had learned that adults could often be taciturn and hold back information for no apparent reason, and I had also discovered that all things eventually become clear to him who watches and waits. Halfway down the inlet Ed nosed *Jove* toward a dock in front of a two-story house with a widow's walk that jutted from the second floor.

I clambered to the bow; as we approached the dock I jumped off with a line. I had been studying from a book of knots until I had mastered several, including the clove hitch and the bowline which I could now tie and undo with my eyes closed. But it was one thing to tie those knots around a tree trunk at leisure and quite another to tie them under duress on a dock. The first time Ed saw me practicing a clove hitch, manipulating standing ends according to the text, he took the line from me and said: "By the time you tie that hitch of yours the boat will have drifted away." Then he showed me how to drop a loop over the top of a mooring post and a second identical loop over the first. Wondrously, the two loops formed a clove hitch, just like that. Now I dropped my two identical loops over the post, caught the stern line Ed tossed me, and did the same. A girl about my own age had come to the dock to observe our maneuvers, and I was careful to act as if I had been dropping clove hitches over mooring posts since I was born.

"Mr. Doubrava," she called. "Daddy would like to talk to you before you start on the Branscomb house."

So it was the Branscomb house we were to set aright. I assumed we were now docked in front of that house— but who was the girl in the halter and shorts with the tanned legs and raspy voice?

"All right, Gwen," Ed said. He walked with her up a

56

boardwalk and entered a house several doors away. He was gone about fifteen minutes. At one point he and another man came down the front steps, walked around the side of the house and disappeared in the reeds. I could see their heads above the spikes on the cattails; they seemed to be inspecting a valued object, a treasure buried in the sand.

"What's going on?" Sara asked.

"I don't know."

"Why don't you ask Ed when he gets back?"

"If he wants us to know, he'll tell us."

"Well then, I'll ask him," Sara said.

"Go ahead. That's fine with me."

But when Ed returned, Sara didn't say a word. She cuddled up in a deck chair with her book as if she were going to read.

Ed went into *Jove*'s cabin and carried out a hefty wooden block with double sheaves and tackle, a bag of cement and a spade. I helped him carry these objects under the Branscomb house where we stood with our knees bent and head bowed to keep from banging our skulls on the overhead beams. Ed climbed to the roof and hung a plumb bob; then he came down and circled the house several times, surveying its lines with a practiced eye. "Never trust a plumb bob," he said. "I've never seen a plumb bob that didn't lie." He studied the peak of the house, the valleys of the roof, the tilt of the porch rails, and at length said, "I'd say she's off perpendicular about four inches, wouldn't you?"

"Seems about right to me."

"But we can only shift her a couple of inches. I don't dare pull her more than that."

He went under the house again and found a place where he could hook the tackle to a supporting post and beam. Then he pulled the heavy rope through the sheaves to the other side of the dwelling and, with the side of his shoe, drew a large rectangle in the sand. "Right there," he said, "I want you to dig a grave six feet deep. Do you think you can?"

"A grave!"

"That's right," he said, "for a deadman."

"A dead man!"

I thought about the furtive way he and his friend, Gwen's father, had disappeared among the cattails, and once again I wondered what they had inspected there. Ed was smiling mysteriously, and for a moment I thought this house-straightening business was a ruse. I thought they had hidden a corpse in the bulrushes and now they were going to bury it in my grave.

I grabbed the spade and started to dig. As the morning passed, I was grateful that I was in the shade under the house, even if I had to stoop, and not outside under the baking sun. Occasionally Sara and Gwen, who had made friends, ambled by on the boardwalk, but I pretended not to notice them. Then Gwen came alone with two bottles of root beer and knelt down under the house in the sand.

"Why are you digging that hole?" she asked.

"It's not a hole," I said. "It's a grave, and it's for a dead man."

"How deep do you plan to dig?"

"Six feet."

"You'll never make it, you know."

I thought she was belittling my stamina and strength. "Of course I will," I said.

"Never," she replied. "When you strike four feet, the water will bubble up. Wait and see." She had a remarkably husky voice, which seemed to come from her chest and give her words a special authority.

"How can you be so sure?"

"I'm sure," she said. "Everybody knows you can't dig more than four feet around here." With that she gathered up the empty bottles and walked away.

As I dug, I could hear Ed rummaging around overhead, searching for rotting timbers and loosened rails. Periodically he would come downstairs and inspect my grave. "Fine, fine," he would say. "Just the right size for a deadman."

It was noon when the bay filled the bottom of my hole. As Gwen had predicted, the grave was four feet deep. Ed rubbed his chin. "All right," he said, "that's deep enough. Let's have some lunch."

Dripping with sweat, I returned to *Jove*, put on my bathing suit and dove from the stern into the inlet, swimming underwater as far as I could. The water was cool here and warm there, and the current was strong and clear. I swam to the center of the channel and then back toward *Jove*. About twenty feet from the dock I stopped, treading water to keep myself afloat. Gwen was sitting on a mooring post at the end of the dock, holding a line which she slowly pulled in, hand over hand.

"What are you fishing for?"

"Eels," she said.

"Don't hook me."

"How could I hook you. My sinker is bouncing on the bottom and you're on the top."

"Besides," I said, "there are no eels here." The idea of an eel slithering about my legs distressed me, but I didn't let on.

"Ha, Mr. Doubrava, he says there are no eels here!"

Ed hoisted himself onto the shed over the cockpit and crouched for an instant, his body poised. Then he arched over the water, cutting the surface like a knife. Sara dove from the coaming and they both swam across the channel. They floated in midstream, and I heard them laughing, but my attention was elsewhere.

"How many eels have you ever caught?" I asked.

"Dozens," she said.

"What do you do with 'em after you catch 'em?"

"Sometimes I bash 'em," she said, "and sometimes I skin 'em alive."

I was intrigued by her cutthroat manner, but I was also filled with an inexplicable sense of dread.

"Do you eat 'em?"

"Of course I eat 'em."

I could no more think of eating an eel than of eating a snake. "I don't believe you."

"You didn't believe you would strike water at four feet either," she said.

Just then her line gave a tremendous jerk, and she yanked it toward her, turning it quickly around a cleat. She whooped and danced on the dock, then retrieved the line until the slimy sea creature dangled in mid-air and floundered helplessly on the planks. She raised a wooden mallet that she kept handy and clouted the eel on the head, but he continued to toss and flop. She raised her club again, set her teeth, and clouted the eel a second time. By then I was out of the water and looking on with excitement and wounded pride at the grisly scene. Gwen picked up the dead eel, squeezing its flat tail between a pair of pliers, and thrust it in my face.

"What do you call that?" she said.

"An eel," I replied.

"An eel, an eel," she taunted me. "Did you ever skin an eel?"

The whole business sounded grotesque, but I was compelled to watch while Gwen took a sharp knife, slit the eel around the head, seized the loose skin with the pliers and turned it inside out, as if she were peeling off a rubber glove. "Tonight," she said, "we'll have eel for supper with onions and peppers. Some for me and some for Sara and some for you."

She dropped the eel in the pail and looked at it with satisfaction. The rays of the sun glistened in her soft brown hair. Suddenly I was filled with a longing that wasn't new, but was more painful and intense than I had ever known before.

After lunch aboard the *Jove*, Ed and I returned to the Branscomb house. Ed laid several boards together beside the grave. We mixed cement and sand, adding water from a bucket that I filled from the kitchen sink. We soon had a slab about two feet thick and six feet long. It was by now clear to me that we would dump the slab in the hole once it had hardened.

"That's the dead man, isn't it?" I said.

"That's the deadman," Ed said.

But if the concrete slab was the deadman, then what was hidden in the cattails beside Gwen's house?

Later that day we tied the rope around the deadman and shoved it into its watery grave. "All right," Ed said, "now fill it in."

The tackle was slack, but Ed pulled on the standing rope until the line was taut. "Come over here," he said, "and lend your weight. Remember, it's like pulling a boat against the current. No sudden jerks! Slow and steady does the job!"

What ensued was a monumental tug-of-war: Ed and I at one end, squatting on the ground and leaning backwards, straining against the inertia of the leaning house. I could hear the timbers groan in protest and then the house relented, shifting a fraction of an inch. After a rest, we resumed the struggle. Each time the house moved Ed would buttress it with two-by-eights. I was astounded at the leverage gained through pulleys, and I saw why it was possible to trim a sail against the awesome weight of the wind. On a sailing vessel, the sheaves are through-bolted to the deck and the boat itself is the deadman.

"That'e enough!" Ed said at last. "If we take the house any further we'll crack the walls."

We went outside and inspected the leaning house. To my dismay, she seemed as lopsided as before. But when I looked closely at the steps, bannisters, railings, I could see the evidence of how far it had actually moved.

"The rest of the job is purely cosmetic," Ed said. He explained that we would return the next day and recut and fasten columns, post and rails so they looked as if they didn't lean. "We can't make the house plumb," he said, "but we can make it look plumb, and that's just as good."

Thus, the straightening of the Branscomb house was partly real and partly illusion, and only Ed and I would know how much it was one and how much the other. Once again the notion of deception crossed my mind. But I saw this wasn't deception; it was the only practical way to proceed.

"The Branscombs will be surprised when they come here and see their house is straight," I said.

"No," Ed said, "they'll be surprised if they come here and find it still leans."

We swam again in the late afternoon, then ate supper at the Gowans. Gwen's mother, a full-faced and cheerful woman, fried the eel in butter with onions and peppers, just as Gwen said she would. To my surprise, I found it delicate and tasty. But Sara picked and poked at it and finally pushed her plate away. Gwen and I split what she left between ourselves.

After supper we sat on the deck in front of the house. Frank Gowan lit a giant cigar.

"Nothing like a good cigar in the early evening," he said, "to keep the mosquitos away."

"The best way to treat mosquitos is to ignore them," Ed volunteered. "Mosquito bites are merely a matter of nerves."

The mosquitos arose from the marsh grass and attacked the back of my neck and legs. Each time I slapped myself, Gwen let out a sultry laugh. After a while I found myself slapping my thighs and arms just to hear the sound of her voice.

63

The sun hung over the westerly tip of the island, setting the marsh aglow. As it descended, the mainland gave up its retained heat, and the once stiff onshore wind dwindled and actually turned, blowing seaward from the shore. Ed and Gwen's father talked of their boyhood, telling tales they had probably told over and over again through their long friendship, and Gwen's mother listened with her hands folded in her lap, pretending she was hearing them for the first time. A purple cloud stretched across the horizon, and that made Gwen's father think of fall.

"In a little while," he said, "the ducks will be coming down the flyway. Then I'll paddle my duckboat over to that distant shore, set out my decoys and settle with my shotgun in a blind among the reeds."

"I don't know if I could shoot a duck," I said. I had never fired a rifle or a shotgun at an animal and I had vowed I never would. But I also knew there were many things I had vowed not to do that I would do before I died.

"Phff, it's not the shooting," Gwen's father said. "It's the waiting in the biting wind and the sight of the ducks flying over the marsh and the wondering if they'll come your way."

The scene Gwen's father painted stirred my imagination. He spoke of sheldrakes and helldivers and butterballs and bluebills—birds I'd never seen. One bleak November day, I thought, I shall sail the fringes of the marshlands and watch for the ducks that winter on the bay.

"Where do you keep the duckboat, anyhow?" Ed asked.

64

"Why," Gwen's father said, "I keep her out of sight in the reeds."

"Let's have a look at her," Ed said. "I'll bet she's all dried out from laying in the sun."

We walked around to the side of the house into the cattails where I had seen the two men disappear earlier that day. There, bottom up in the tall grass, was a sharp-prowed boat with a wood hull painted green, about 14 feet long.

"Just as I thought," Ed said. "You can see daylight through her seams."

"Well," Gwen's father explained, "I only use her now in the fall."

"She sure seems sound," I said.

"I had her built for sailing," Gwen's father said, "but I don't sail much anymore. But she works out fine as a duckboat."

"Why don't we drag her down to the water," Ed said, "and see how much she swells."

"She'll swell up tight as a drum in forty-eight hours," Gwen's father said. "You can count on that."

"I bet she will," Ed said.

My heart was thumping now, but I knew there was an unspoken etiquette among men like these. Don't ask questions. Let things happen as they may!

The three of us pushed the boat down an embankment into the shallow water and tied her to the dock. She was a shoal-draft, V-bottomed sloop with a long centerboard trunk. She floated freely as the water seeped through her open seams.

"Anytime you want to sail her," Gwen's father said, "that's all right with me."

"What about spars," I said. "Does she have spars?" I knew she must have spars and rigging, for she had a step for her mast and fastenings for her stays.

"Boom, mast, rigging and rudder are all under the house," Gwen said.

"She's going to need some caulking around the trunk," Ed said, "and a little fixing here and there."

I sat on the edge of the dock and Gwen sat beside me, so close our thighs touched. I watched the sloop fill slowly with water until her deck was level with the bay.

"Will she sink?" Gwen asked.

"Of course not," I said. "She won't sink because she has no keel to drag her down. She'll fill with water but she'll still float like a rowboat or a canoe."

"Tomorrow," she said, "you'll have to bail her out."

"But does she really sail?" I asked.

Two days later, after work, I boarded the sloop with a bucket and a coffee can and bailed her out. For a while it seemed as if the seawater was still coming in as fast as I poured it out, but the boat was rising toward her waterline a little at a time. After an hour or so, the sloop was riding on the water the way she was meant to. But I could still see dampness around her centerboard trunk.

Ed came along with some caulking cotton and stuffed it into the opening around the trunk, making her tight. Then he removed a number of rusted screws and bolts and put fresh ones in. Finally, we carried the spars down to the dock and rigged her, just to see how she looked with mast, boom and stays in place.

"She's not the prettiest boat in the world," Ed said. "But she'll do."

66

"She's no longer a duckboat," I said. "Now she's a sloop."

That night aboard *Jove* I lay awake in the upper starboard berth. Ed was asleep below me and Sara, breathing easily, was also asleep, on the port side. Through a porthole I could see my sloop swaying gently in the dying wind under the light of the moon. My thoughts leaped from the boat to Gwen and back to the boat again as I tried to suppress a disturbing thought. I had the boat and I had the spars and I had the rigging, but they were all useless to me, for I had no sails.

4

Aunt Flo atoned for her sins with her hands. When she wasn't cooking and cleaning, she was making new clothes for Sara or darning the heels and toes of my socks, which were always filled with holes. She rarely bought store clothes and she never threw anything away.

But every day between three and four in the afternoon Aunt Flo would put aside her cares and play the piano. She was a fine musician. She was also a firm believer in self-discipline and she practiced religiously. She said that playing the piano was her one pleasure in life, but I was skeptical. Playing the piano seemed yet another punishment she inflicted on herself.

She gave piano lessons to Sara and, for a time, to me. Sara had a superb ear and could pick out popular tunes on the keyboard, which was the only thing that interested me and the one thing I couldn't do. Nevertheless, Aunt Flo made me play *"Tweedledum and Tweedledee"* over and over again, hoping that through constant repetition I might eventually get it right. "If you learn to read music," she would say, "then you can play whatever you like." But I didn't want to read music; I wanted to play by ear or not at all.

Sara would laugh at my attempts to make both hands strike the right chords at the same time. Recognizing the impossibility of it all, I would laugh too, and make deliberate mistakes, hoping Aunt Flo would abandon her mission of trying to make a musician of me. Usually Aunt Flo would overlook our merriment, but when her migraine was coming on she would threaten to punish us both unless we showed more self-discipline and practiced as we should.

Aunt Flo was a perfectionist, and she had a favorite story about the genius painter and sculptor, Michelangelo, that emphasized her point. Michelangelo, according to her story, had sculpted a statue for a wealthy patron that stood against a wall in the patron's villa. The statue had a minor flaw, but it was around the back against the wall, where it couldn't be seen. Nevertheless, Michelangelo set about correcting that flaw, which haunted him. One day the patron saw him fixing the flaw and said, "Michelangelo, what are you doing? That flaw is quite minor and it can't be seen. Why nobody even knows it's there!"

"Ah," said Michelangelo, "but I know it's there."

And Aunt Flo knew we were there, and the minor defects in our musicianship made her wince. One day while we were convulsed in laughter over a silly mistake, she actually threatened us with a strap she had brought from her bedroom and Sara went white with fear. But I stared at her as if she were someone I barely knew. I knew her head was throbbing and she was too weak to raise her arms.

"You're ungrateful children," she said, "both of you, and you don't have any appreciation for what you have." With that, she collapsed in her bed and remained there for three days.

Aunt Flo believed she had an obligation to expose Sara and me to the higher things in life. She and Uncle Bert belonged to a musical society that met monthly in the home of a member. Aunt Flo accompanied the soloist, a soprano named Gertrude Verplanck, a buxom woman who reeked of cheap perfume.

Whenever the musicale was in our house, Aunt Flo made Sara and me sit in the kitchen, where we couldn't be seen but where we could hear every note. We would take turns peeking through the kitchen door and mimicking the oboist. But when Miss Verplanck sang we would retreat behind the refrigerator and cover our mouths with our hands.

"Oh yes, Mommy," Sara would say when, at long last, the guests went home, "it was a lovely musicale."

"And wasn't Trudy just grand?" Aunt Flo would say.

"Oh yes, Mommy, Trudy sang beautifully tonight."

Gertrude Verplanck was also guest soloist at the local Christian Science Church where every Sunday Uncle Bert passed the collection plate and Aunt Flo accompanied the soprano on a marvelous pipe organ that filled one wall. My parents had raised me a heathen, and until I joined the Mann household I had never seen the inside of a church. I had grown up thinking Sunday morning was the time God had set aside to sleep off the ill effects of the night before. But the Manns, who didn't smoke or drink, disapproved of the dissolute life my parents led. Aunt Flo let me know that my irreligion was a state she intended to change. "As your guardians," she said, "we will give you a religion until you are old enough to choose your own."

Sara and I went regularly to Christian Science Sunday School where I learned that sickness and death were sins I could overcome with perfect love. For years thereafter I regarded my recurrent hayfever as a special kind of wickedness and felt downright despicable whenever I was sick. Then one day my high school biology teacher told me my sensitivity to ragweed pollen was probably an inherited trait locked in my genes. I blamed my allergy on my unknown ancestors and felt better right away.

But something good came from that Sunday School, for we read Biblical passages with interpretations from *Science and Health with Key to the Scriptures* by Mary Baker Eddy, founder of the sect. The interpretations I dismissed as obtuse, but the passionate stories from the King James version awoke within me a sense of literature that never waned. I would read aloud moving and poetical passages about retribution, envy, lust, greed, unbridled ambition and imperfect earthly love.

But how often were my recitations interrupted by the sound of the organ in the worship room overhead and then the flat, ringing voice of Gertrude Verplanck? Sara and I, who weren't in the same class, would glance at each other across the large room and instinctively put our hands to our mouths.

There was a third sister, Aunt Claudia, who played the piano too. Aunt Claudia was six years younger than Aunt Flo and two years younger than my mother, but she had already been married three times: first to a rich furrier with a glass eye, then to an underworld figure who was shot to death in Detroit and, finally, to a madcap artist who refused to work. This last husband, an avowed Communist, would strut around the Mann's house and criticize my father's "bourgois" paintings, which hung on the walls. "They stink of sentimentality," he would say, which I suppose they did. But I worshipped them all the same.

"Peter darling," Aunt Claudia would say to him, "stop this silliness and leave my pussycat alone!"

Aunt Claudia didn't care for Sara. "She walks around all the time with a long face," Aunt Claudia would say. But I was her pussycat and she would play the piano for me. She had a fine ear and a delicate touch. When she played, her long painted fingernails clicked along the keyboard and her bracelets jangled, but I could still feel the sorrow that filled her days.

"Oh Claudia, Claudia," Aunt Flo would say, "if you would only practice—you can play so well!"

But Aunt Claudia had no time to practice. She was too busy searching for a man to look after her and always latching on to husbands who abused her in the worst way.

The two sisters told terrible tales about each other. Aunt Flo said that when Claudia was young she went out on dates without her underpants. Aunt Claudia said that when Flo was a girl my grandfather, an erratic tyrant, would lock her in a clothes closet whenever she misbehaved. One time he heard disgusting noises coming from the closet and called out:

"Flo, what are you doing in there?" To which Aunt

Flo replied, "I'm spitting and I'm spitting and now I'm waiting for more spit!"

I loved Aunt Claudia and looked forward expectantly to her infrequent visits. But she never stayed long, mainly because she was addicted to cigarettes and whenever she wanted to smoke Aunt Flo made her go into the bathroom and lock the door.

Shortly after we moved into our new house, my piano lessons stopped. The compulsive energy Aunt Flo previously poured into her piano she now diverted to her sewing machine. Beset by bills, she decided to open a dressmaking shop. Uncle Bert tried to talk her out of it.

"Flossie, Flossie," he pointed out, "you can't make enough. Can't you see?" Then he would go over the figures again—so much for rent, so much for utilities, so much for a sewing machine, so much for scissors, thimbles and thread. "It's impossible," he would say. "I won't allow it."

But when Aunt Flo decided to sacrifice herself on the altar of her family, there was no stopping her. In truth, her acts hardly qualified as sacrifices because no benefit accrued elsewhere. If Agamemnon throws his daughter over the cliff, he does so with the expectation that he will appease the gods and the winds will blow. But if the winds fail to blow, then he commits only a senseless slaughter that will torment him all his days.

Fortunately for Agamemnon, the winds blew. But for Aunt Flo there was only self-denial with no commensurate gain. Her sacrifices began in guilt and ended in futility. As I grew older Uncle Bert would say to me, as if I were a disinterested party: "Don't think too badly of her. She means well." He wanted me to know there was nothing he could do.

On rare occasions he would face her down. Then she would turn on him and tell him he wasn't a man. "If you were a man," she would say, "then you would be a provider. But you don't provide, so you're not a man. You're a jellyfish, that's what you are!"

"Flo," he would protest, "how can you say that, what do you mean." He would attempt to defend himself by explaining rationally why our finances weren't as desperate as she made them out to be. But it was useless, for Aunt Flo was possessed by demon fears he couldn't dispel.

One day, distraught by her vision of mounting debts, she threatened to leave, to go to the home of a second cousin who lived nearby. Uncle Bert, mortified at the thought that she would take her troubles to a distant relative, seized her by the shoulders as she tried to rush out the door without so much as a change of clothes. While he was dragging her back into the house, she was pummeling him on the chest and kicking him in the shins. Sara screamed at them both, imploring them to stop. I felt myself go numb. "They aren't a part of me," I said to myself, "and I'm not a part of them." I believe my emotional distance saved me, for I could see that Sara, who couldn't detach herself, was becoming increasingly morose. But I paid a severe penalty for my estrangement.

Uncle Bert disliked confrontations and usually he wouldn't allow a situation to go that far. It was easier to let Aunt Flo open her dressmaker's shop than engage in a prolonged struggle that ended in bitterness. At such moments I would conclude that Aunt Flo was right. Uncle Bert was a jellyfish after all.

Aunt Flo opened her dressmaking shop in leased space over the Five and Dime downtown. Customers entered through a glass door on Main Street to which Aunt Flo had her name affixed in gold lettering:

FLORENCE MANN
DRESSMAKING & ALTERATIONS

Access to the shop was up a narrow flight of stairs. Because the shop was in the center of a small town, everyone knew immediately that Aunt Flo had opened a business of her own and concluded that Uncle Bert had come upon hard times.

The shop itself was divided into two rooms, one large one for working and one small one for changing clothes. The larger room contained a sewing machine, a dressmaker's dummy set on a metal stanchion, and a large tabletop supported on a pair of sawhorses and strewn with fabrics. But the shop's most notable characteristic was the reprehensible odor of stale perfume worn by Aunt Flo's patrons.

The shop had three windows. Two were in the front, overlooking the Main Street shopping district, which was about five blocks long in those days, extending from a movie house at one end to a drug store at the other. The third window was in the rear and it overlooked a parking lot and the creek, oily and filled with debris at this end, that flowed past Ed Doubrava's house toward the bay.

75

Whenever I entered I would raise the back window to let in the sea breeze.

At first I avoided the shop altogether, but after I acquired sailing rights to Frank Gowan's duckboat I stopped by every day. I would sit with my back to the open window and watch how Aunt Flo ran her sewing machine. I saw how she threaded the bobbin and stitched the fabric and pushed her knee against the extended bar under the table to start the needle whirring like a pneumatic drill.

Occasionally Sara would go with me, but after a while she pretended the dressmaking shop didn't exist and her mother had departed on an extended trip to the ends of the world. The dressmaking shop was a source of anguish for Sara, for many of her mother's customers were also the mothers of her friends. If one of Sara's friends mentioned that Aunt Flo was making a dress for her mother, Sara would turn the conversation aside as if she hadn't heard a word.

"Why does she do it, Rick?" she would say to me in private. "Why! Why!"

"I don't know Sara. I wish I knew."

"Daddy is dead set against it."

"I know, Sara. I know."

"He says she doesn't even make her expenses. It's actually costing him money to have her run her . . . her . . ." Sara couldn't finish; she couldn't accept the fact that her mother was the local dressmaker and was pinning up other people's hems.

One day I pulled my chair as close as possible to the sewing machine and watched Aunt Flo sew a seam, totally absorbed. Then, sensing my nearness, she looked up and said, "What ails you, anyhow?"

"Aunt Flo," I said, "I want to ask you a favor."

She turned off her machine and looked at me in surprise, for I don't think I had ever asked her for a favor before. It never occurred to me that she might be waiting for me to ask, as if it were a sign that I accepted her.

"What would you like?" she asked.

"I want to use your sewing machine," I said.

Aunt Flo's notions about my handiness resulted from her watching me hit piano keys, and I knew even before I asked that she would never let me near her precious sewing machine.

"What on earth for?"

"I want to make a sail. Two sails, in fact. A jib and a mainsail."

"A jib and a mainsail?"

"Yes. One fits aft of the mast and the other . . ."

"Never mind that. Why you don't even have any sail cloth!"

"I thought I could use the money I earned working for Ed and buy something used down at the sailmakers. They say Egyptian cotton is the best."

"Egyptian cotton. For pity's sake, Rick, that's expensive material."

Having made that point, she hunched over, pressed her knee against the starter bar and I heard the rat-a-tat of the needle once more. Whenever Sara wanted something, she nagged away, and I was wondering if now Aunt Flo expected me to do the same. But I had resolved that regardless of how much I wanted my sails I wouldn't imitate Sara. I would ask once and that was all.

After several minutes, Aunt Flo, seeing that I wasn't about to pursue the matter, turned off her machine for the second time.

"Do you really mean to sail that duckboat, or whatever it is?" she said.

"I'd like to, Aunt Flo. Ed says it's perfectly safe."

"All you seem to think about are boats. Boats, boats—that's all you have on your mind."

I didn't care what she said as long as she didn't start sewing again as if I weren't there. She mulled the matter for a while, then added, "Of course, it's perfectly natural, I suppose. I have nothing against your sailing. It's just that sailing can be expensive and we're having trouble making ends meet right now."

"I understand, Aunt Flo," I said. "I don't want you to spend any money. I just thought I could find some suitable material somewhere and then stitch it together on your sewing machine."

"We'll talk about it some more after supper," she said, and she went back to work.

She was as good as her word. After supper that same night we went down into the cellar where she had squirreled away every possession she or Uncle Bert or Sara had ever owned. There was a tricycle down there, a doll's house with tiny dolls, a spinning top and rusty tools. There were old suits, dresses, scarves, gloves and stained ties. Everything was neatly marked and stacked in boxes, for Aunt Flo couldn't bear to throw anything away. "Who knows when you'll need these things, or your children will need them," she would say. But years later, when Sara and I had children of our own, Aunt Flo held on to her tricycles, doll houses and dolls. To the best of my knowledge, she never gave up anything from her cellar storehouse—except what she gave me that day.

She went to a large cedar chest and removed an old woven bedspread, nearly threadbare.

"How about that?" she said.

"Aunt Flo," I said, "it's lovely, it really is. But it will stretch too much."

Then she removed some old sheets.

"How about these?" she said.

"I don't think so," I said.

"What do you mean 'I don't think so!' That's fine percale!"

"But it's so sheer, Aunt Flo. One good blow and it will rip for sure."

"You certainly are fussy," she said.

She pulled all her accumulated linens from the cedar chest until, way down near the bottom, she found an orange awning that used to hang across the back porch at the old bungalow. It was slightly mildewed, but stiff and strong, and I could see at once that it could be cut up into a crazy patchwork pattern to form a suit of sails.

"Aunt Flo," I said, "that's perfect."

"Well, it's not perfect," she said, "but it will do."

During the following week she found time every day to piece together my sail to the dimensions I had brought home with me after carefully measuring the spars. She overlapped the canvas edges, tucked them under on each side and stitched them so they wouldn't part. She sewed metal grommets into the tack, clew and head of the mainsail and along its luff so that I could attach it to the main halyard, boom and mast. She even made crude batten pockets although she had no idea what I meant when I said I needed them to keep the roach stiff. From the excess material she fashioned a jib with snaps so that I could attach it to the forestay. It was arduous labor—both for her and her sewing machine. She broke many needles, but she persevered.

While she worked, I sat with a notebook in my lap, my back to the open window and a soft breeze on my neck, and composed a poem. I had taken to writing verse in my spare time, constructing crude iambic stanzas with complex rhyme schemes and stuffing them in my desk drawer. But I intended this one to see the light of day. I called it "To My Sailmaker," and when Aunt Flo finished my sail I gave her my poem, although it hardly seemed a fair exchange.

She sat by her sewing machine, her lips trembling as she read. "You mean you wrote this?" she said. "You mean you wrote this poem for me." When she finished she took my hand and held it to her breast and wept as though she would never be consoled. I stood there foolishly, not knowing what to do. It was as if nobody had ever treated her with affection or touched her deeply before.

The wind at mid-morning was light, a trickling stream that drifted across the sand spit from the ocean. We hoisted sails and I expected Ed would take the tiller on this trial run, but he told me to sit at the helm and steer while he tended the jib sheets. I waded in shallow water along the shore, aware that Gwen, ever present, was watching from the dock. Josie and Evelyn, Aunt Flo, Uncle Bert and Sara were absorbed in their private affairs aboard *Jove*.

I leaned against the stern, guiding the sloop toward deeper water, and then leaped aboard after a final push. For an instant there was no wind, and then it was there, filling my orange canvas. I had an anxious moment, for everything about this converted duckboat was makeshift, and I had no idea how she would respond.

Her mainsail was tied with twine to metal rings that slid up and down her mast. Her jib, which had no battens, was far too small, for there wasn't enough of Aunt Flo's discarded awning to go around. Her rudder wobbled on rusty runners screwed into the transom. Her sheets and halyards were frayed hemp from *Jove*'s storage locker. Her centerboard had swelled so tightly inside her warped trunk that Ed had to forcibly shove it down with an oar.

But, for all that, she sailed.

She heeled slightly and we skimmed across the surface like a skater on thin ice, so smoothly that it hardly seemed as if we made headway. But the gentle wind raised tiny ripples on the water and the weathered houses slipped past along the shore.

"Head upwind!" Ed ordered and I had to translate his command, for the touch of the tiller hadn't yet become a matter of instinct with me. I groped for more familiar words, like a stranger in a foreign land. "To swing the bow to starboard, push the tiller to port"—that's what I had to say to myself. I understood the fluid mechanics of water swirling past a slanted rudder, but I hadn't entered that holy place in which the boat and I were one.

We sailed close-hauled, the boom at an acute angle to the deck and the bow pointing down the narrow estuary, which led to the westernmost tip of the island. Then we veered north over shoals and flats on a broad reach. There was no sign of human habitation, except for a beached dory abandoned to the elements, its hull bleached to driftwood by the salt and sun. I had often read stories about blue-water sailors who defied the seas. They were always being trapped in squalls or dashed against rocks or becalmed for weeks like the Ancient Mariner with his endless tale of the albatross. But I had never read about the romance of sailing in two feet of water so close to the marsh you could hear the saltwind rustling in the reeds.

We were running now with a brisk and building wind behind. The boom hung at right angles to the surging sloop; the mainsail was filled but the jib luffed ineffectually, sometimes billowing and then collapsing again. Once, during Race Week, I had seen sleek sloops with whisker poles that ran from the mast to the clew of the jib; the poles held the foresail out squarely across the bow where it could catch the breeze.

"If we had a whisker pole," I said, "we could really move."

"You don't need a whisker pole," Ed replied. He told me to trim the slack jib sheet on the windward deck and, at the same time, head another notch off the wind. As I did, the jib began to draw, and we were scudding along, mainsail to port and jib to starboard, wing and wing.

With a following breeze, the lowered centerboard was a useless drag. Ed leaned forward and raised the board, which was scraping the sandy bottom. Before he could straighten up, a fleeting image caught his eye under the sail. He pointed and I saw a slender bird with a black back and white forked tail gliding off the bow. The bird skimmed inches above the surface and then dipped its lower bill into the water, leaving a thin wake, the sole trace of its passage. Then I saw a second bird skimming the surface, scooping baitfish into its long red bill. This one flew strongly and gracefully like its mate. It seemed to me as if there weren't separate worlds for birds and men, but one world in which both species rely on the same wind and tide.

"Scissor-bills," Ed said, squinting into the sun, memory lining his face. "They were here when I was just a kid. They've been here for a million years, I guess."

The only sound was the swish of the hull as she soared downwind. The duckboat had a strong weather helm, and as she surged to windward of her own volition I had to pull the tiller to leeward to keep both sails filled.

"Careful now!" Ed said. "Don't get lulled into a false sense of security! Going with the wind seems so nice and easy—but it's the most dangerous course of all. Head too far upwind and your jib will flap—that's not too bad! But head too far off the wind and you'll accidentally jibe!"

I knew what he meant, for Neil and I had jibed more than once without intending to. One moment we were coasting downwind without a care, and the next instant the boom was crashing across the cockpit, narrowly missing our skulls.

When my sloop veered upwind, I deliberately let the jib collapse. Ed smiled at my conservative instincts, but he offered no further advice. Here was a delicate balance between speed and safety, something I would have to learn for myself.

At the eastern tip of the island we headed south on a

broad reach again. Suddenly I was maneuvering in deep water amid the state boat channel with power craft bearing down on every side. Ahead, I had the steep wake of a boat that crossed my bow; behind I had a skiff bent on running me down astern. In the distance were a half-dozen boats of varying size, all seemingly on a collision course with mine.

Sensing my confusion, Ed said: "Hold your course, you're doing fine. One thing at a time!"

The wake of the crossing cabin cruiser struck our forward quarter on the starboard, sending up a fine spray. The duckboat rose easily over the first wave, dipped and rose again over the second wave and plowed right through the third wave, her deck awash, before entering placid seas once more. We had shipped a small amount of water, that was all. The boat behind cut her engines as she passed and I eased between the spreading waves in her gentle wake, following directly behind. As for all those other boats, they didn't come within a hundred yards.

The wind, which had risen slightly west of south, was now due southwest and steady, and I had to tack upwind along the estuary past the summer homes toward *Jove*. Both Ed and I hiked up on the windward deck as the sloop heeled. Sometimes I would ease the mainsail and sometimes I would head up, but I could feel the confidence rise within me as I sailed. I was exultant, for I had circumnavigated an island, my hand on the tiller every inch of the way.

But now I had to perform the most precise maneuver of our island journey. Ed told me to head up into the wind alongside *Jove*, nosing up on her port side. For some reason, I overshot my mark and came straight at *Jove* amidships like a torpedo. Then, instead of instinctively pushing the tiller toward the mainsail I pulled it toward myself as I sat high on the windward deck. The boat gathered speed and her sharp-nosed prow—covered with a piece of protective metal—drove into *Jove*'s hull. There was a dull thud and the sound of cracking wood as the sloop stove a hole in the planking above the waterline.

I had had the same sinking feeling once before when I was very small. I had mistakenly taken one of my father's commercial drawings and, placing it in the middle of the living room floor, crayoned over the top in that special scribble that makes sense only to a child. Suddenly I felt myself being lifted unceremoniously into the air. There was a moment of awful suspense as I realized I had done something wrong, and then I was being lowered safely to the floor once more.

My mother, hearing my father's groan, came rushing into the room. "What's the matter!" she said, and then she looked to where he was pointing at his ruined painting. She stared dumbly, and then burst out laughing and my father started laughing too.

"I suppose it was my own fault," he said. "I always give him my used drawing boards—so how was he to know!"

Ed ran his hand over his damaged hull. "It's not beyond repair," he said, and then he turned to me, annoyance and amusement mingling in his eyes.

"What happened?" he asked.

"I'm sorry," I said. "At the last minute I got confused and pulled the tiller the wrong way."

"You sure did," he said. "Well, we can't let that happen again, can we?"

He pulled the boat ashore, cut off a huge chunk of rubber from a worn tire that served as a fender against the dock, and nailed the bumper over the metal bow. "Now," he said, "the next time you ram something you'll bounce off like a rubber ball."

The Manns and Stritches were visiting with the Gowans when the ramming occurred, but Gwen had witnessed the entire mishap from her position on the dock.

"That was a crackerjack landing, Rick," she said to me, giving my right arm a thumping wallop with her fist. At times I wished she were a boy.

"Why don't you take Gwen for a sail now," Ed said, "while I see what I can do about that gaping hole." I knew then that he was going to make some quick, temporary repairs at dockside and never tell Aunt Flo and Uncle Bert about what I had done. I was grateful for that, for I knew Uncle Bert would offer to pay for repairs and that would set off a new round of feuding about family finances.

I guess that Ed's income was no greater than Uncle Bert's and might even be less. Yet Ed seemed to be able to take from life exactly what he wanted while Uncle Bert constantly struggled against the odds and never acquired what gave him happiness.

There were two different kinds of people in the world, I thought. There were those like Ed for whom work and pleasure were all one piece, and there were those like Uncle Bert who worked and bought their pleasures from someone else. They were breeds apart, those two, and sometime during the course of growing up a boy decides —whether he knows it or not—which of the two he wants to be.

"Can you sail?" I said to Gwen.

"Not really."

"Well, don't worry. I'll teach you."

I pushed the boat offshore. As we cut across the channel, a notion entered my head.

"Why don't we inspect that abandoned dory," I said, "the one that washed up on the beach?"

"Okay," she said, letting the jib sheet go on one side and trimming it on the other as we came about. Her timing was perfect.

"So you do know how to sail," I said.

"A little."

"Would you like to take the tiller?"

"I'm afraid we might capsize."

I knew she was lying. She wouldn't have been afraid if a leviathan rose from the depths and wrapped itself around our hull. She would've clobbered the sea serpent with her club. Yet I was dissembling too—pretending I wasn't affected by being alone in a boat with her. I didn't know what I was supposed to do about this anguish that adults dismiss with a laugh, calling it infatuation and puppy love.

Now the breeze blew stiffer than ever out of the west and I could see whitecaps kicking up to the north across the bay. We jibed deliberately, raised the centerboard and planed across the shoals with a brisk wind at our backs. When the hull scraped bottom, Gwen jumped off the bow with the end of the jib sheet, which she had turned around a cleat. She planted her feet firmly in the sand and eased the nose of the duckboat into the wind.

She was strong and agile—for a girl. But she was a girl.

I threw a small mushroom anchor overboard and secured the end of the anchor rode around the mast. The sloop swung freely at her mooring, always tending into the wind. We let the sails luff and waded ashore, the water clear and warm against our legs.

Suddenly Gwen reached down and plucked a periwinkle from the bottom and held it in her hand. She was forever fetching strange animals from the depths, and I never knew what she was going to haul up next. She had an affinity for the creatures under the sea, and she was herself a mysterious creature—and that was part of her allure. She knew where to tred for clams, where to locate hermit crabs, where to net blue claws against the pilings under the dock. She found whelks and mussels and razor clams and, of course, she was fully versed in the ways of the eel.

"Let's see him," I said, and she placed the small shell in my hand. I touched the rubbery foot and the snail snuggled more deeply into its shell. "Is he good eating?"

"You are an idiot," she said and splashed water in my face.

I put the periwinkle back on the bay bottom and in the same motion seized her ankle, raised her leg and dumped her over in the shallows on her back. When she recovered she slugged my arm again in the same place as before. Then she was running toward deeper water with me in pursuit. We plunged into the channel where we grappled and I dunked her again.

"Maybe she is a boy, after all," I said to myself as we

88

thrashed about, meaning that I could treat her as a boy. But even as the idea crossed my mind I knew it couldn't be so. A sweetness filled my body, an inescapable tenderness. This wasn't a test of strength, but an excuse to explore the borders of the unknown.

She called a truce and I pulled her with both hands up the embankment and back into the shoals. We waded with the late August sun at our backs until we reached the dory which had been deserted to the elements no one knew how many summers before.

"It's in worse shape than I thought," I said.

"Daddy said it washed up here one day after a spring storm and it's been here ever since."

We climbed over the rotting gunwale and sat inside. Our bodies were still wet and the hot sand clung to our legs, arms and hands. Inside the abandoned boat, we were barricaded from the world.

"Do you like Sara?" Gwen asked.

"Sara is my cousin," I said. It hardly seemed an answer, but it told Gwen something she wanted to know.

"You're not a Mann," she said.

"That's right. I'm a Bode," I said, and told her how I came to live with the Manns.

"But Sara," she said, "she's a Mann?"

Sometimes my friends would refer to Aunt Flo as my mother and I always felt compelled to set them straight. "You don't mean my mother," I would say, "you mean my aunt." But there were other times when I deplored this division, for it seemed to set me apart, and I wished it didn't exist.

"I think of Sara as my sister," I said. "But she's not really my sister."

"But you like her as a sister?"

"Yes, of course."

"Then how do you like me?" she said, and a fearful chill swept through my bones even though we were protected from the wind.

"A lot," I said. I hadn't expected her to ask a question like that so directly, but her directness also appealed to me. "I like you a lot," I said as a momentary gust swirled through our barricade.

She closed her eyes and leaned forward and I wanted to brush my lips against her lips, her hair, but I found I couldn't move. I was afraid that if I touched her now she would melt into the sand and wash out with the tide.

After a while she opened her eyes again and looked at me, hurt. "What's the matter?" she asked softly, unable to understand.

"Nothing Gwen."

She climbed out of the dory and waded to the sloop. I followed, knowing somehow I would have to find my way out of this tangled morass of futile memories. We sailed home without a word.

5 ~

In the days that followed, I saw the blue sloop many times. She appeared as a regal spectator at regattas, not deigning to test herself against the fleet. She loomed on the horizon near the Fire Island Light while I trolled for bluefish from the stern of *Jove.* She swept past the shoals where I treaded waist deep in the still bay waters for chowder clams. She was always aloof, like a lovely lady who knows but never acknowledges that she is being admired from afar.

All that summer and the next I sailed my duckboat among the islands that dot the lee shore. As *Jove* approached the Gowan dock, I would look about for Gwen, but I rarely saw her anymore. Her eeling days seemed to have come to an end. Although I often heard her hoarse voice inside her house, she never came out on the dock when I was around. Occasionally I would tell myself to knock on the screen door and ask for her, but I always convinced myself I didn't really care. I would rather raise my sails and cruise toward a secret cove for a rendezvous with *Jove.*

One day I asked Aunt Flo if she wanted to sail with me. To my astonishment, she readily agreed. There was a light morning breeze; even so, I hugged the shore. I didn't want to arouse her anxiety about capsizing in water over her head.

"It's quite safe along here," I said. "We won't tip. But if we do, you can stand on the bottom with no trouble at all."

"I'm not worried about tipping," she said. "You know, Rick, I was a strong swimmer when I was a girl."

"Were you, Aunt Flo?"

"Yes, I was. I swam two miles every day when I was your age."

"Two miles!" I was impressed. Two miles was more than a third of the way across the bay from the Brightwaters Canal to the Lighthouse. "Where was that, Aunt Flo?"

"Jamaica Bay."

I thought she was talking about the island of Jamaica. "In the Caribbean?"

"No, no! On the south shore of Brooklyn, beside the Rockaways."

The Rockaways—the name had a familiar ring. Then I recalled reading newspaper stories about studies to reclaim a body of water near the Rockaways—or perhaps build a large airport there when the war was over. If it ever would be over. Every night I listened to the somber voice of Edward R. Murrow reporting from a bombed-out building somewhere in battered London. It was nightmarish. But here on the bay there was only a delicate breeze and tranquil skies.

"That must've been a long time ago."

"Oh yes, before the war." She was silent for a while, as if she were trying to remember what it was like to be a girl and swim so far. For a moment I was puzzled by her statement, and then I realized she wasn't talking about the present war but about that other war that took place before I was born. She was talking about ancient history—1910 or so.

I tried to imagine Aunt Flo back then, as I studied her build and concluded she was telling the truth. Although she was small, she had the thick chest and strong arms of a swimmer. Unlike Uncle Bert, she had no fear of the water. Sailing aboard my duckboat, she didn't seem like Aunt Flo at all.

I wondered what happened to people as they grew old. How was it that Aunt Flo, who once swam for miles in Jamaica Bay, was now afflicted with wracking migraines that sent her to bed for days at a time? I wondered if such a thing could happen to me, and I concluded that it couldn't. In my innocence, I assumed I would always be hiking to windward with the summer sun burning my neck.

"Of course," Aunt Flo said, "most people won't swim that far. It's not that they can't—it's that they're afraid. Your mother, you know, she loved to swim too. But Aunt Claudia was afraid of the water. She would race up and down the beach, terrified by the waves. She would shout at your Grandpa and tell him I was swimming out too far. Your Grandpa would always sit in the sand, fully dressed in a white shirt and dark pants, with a whistle hanging from a lanyard around his neck. Whenever Aunt Claudia summoned him, he would walk down to the water's edge and blow his whistle. When I heard the piercing whistle, I knew I had swum too far and it was time to turn around."

I had the feeling that she could still hear the piercing whistle in her inner ear. "But the main thing," I said, "is that you weren't afraid."

"No," she said, "in those days I wasn't afraid."

She was sitting on a boat cushion, scrunched between the centerboard trunk and the deck. She could see over the stern, and I don't think anything escaped her notice along the shore, in the water, or aboard the boat. Yet she seemed more at peace with herself than at any time since I arrived so unexpectedly on that fateful day after my parents died. I felt we were coming to an understanding: she could never be my mother and I could never be her son. That wasn't an end, but a beginning, a base on which to build.

She asked about the sloop—how it steered, how it sailed, how it moved, as if for the first time she saw in it an element of self-mastery born of helmsmanship. I explained as best I could, allowing my voice now and again to adopt the intonations of authority. But she seemed to realize that the physics of sailing reveals very little about the art. She fell silent again, closed her eyes and listened to the swishing of the water against the hull.

Most of the time, however, Aunt Flo stayed aboard *Jove* while Sara sailed with me. At first Sara shunned the converted duckboat, as if it were beneath her dignity to be seen aboard such a raffish craft. After all, what was she but a leaky sieve with peeling green deck paint and patchwork orange sails. She was as disreputable as Cinderella before the ball.

But gradually Sara's natural aversion gave way to her

acquisitive instincts and she began to claim the rights of co-ownership. She started to call the duckboat "our sloop." (We both tended to forget, of course, that neither of us owned the boat; she belonged to Gwen's father and we enjoyed her on borrowed time.) I worked on the theory that a sloop belongs to the person who can sail her. Since Sara couldn't sail, she really wasn't "our sloop" at all. She was my sloop. Sara was at my mercy. We sailed only when I said so.

But I didn't press my advantage too far, for I knew I would need Sara as an ally if I were to acquire a real sloop of my own. I never let her forget that she had promised to use her wiles on her father to induce him to buy a boat for me someday. Now it occurred to me that I had a much better chance of getting that boat if Sara wanted it as much as I. She was far more likely to agitate Uncle Bert on her own behalf than mine. So I gave her half the duckboat; it seemed to me a minor concession in the interest of a greater gain. All I had to do now was convince her that she wanted a sloop, had to have a sloop or she would die. In this matter I was as calculating as a businessman.

Then one day Sara saw the blue sloop too. It happened this way.

Ed had dropped us off at Gowan's dock and told us to sail the duckboat around Captree Island into the deepwater channel that led toward Fire Island inlet. He said he would anchor *Jove* off Democrat Point and wait for us there. It was a treacherous journey, but Ed figured the tide was coming in and we would be beating against the wind, so there was little chance of our drifting out to sea.

We sailed on a close reach through the state boat channel where the traffic was especially heavy that day. Most of the time we seemed to be plowing through the wakes of charter fishing boats, which Sara found most disagreeable. She couldn't quite reconcile herself to the fact that the charter boats had as much right to the waterway as we. She kept ducking from side to side, complaining about the cold salt spray. Her constant fidgeting made it difficult for me to keep the boat on even keel.

"When you sail, you're bound to get wet sometimes," I said.

"That's fine for you to say," she shot back, "but I just washed my hair."

"A little salt is good for the scalp," I said. "It kills the dandruff."

"I don't have dandruff!" she said. "Who says I have dandruff!"

"Sara," I said, "if you don't stop bouncing around, you're going to have salt in a lot of other places besides your hair."

"This is such a nasty little boat," she said. "I hate it. I really do. It doesn't have a dry spot in it anywhere!"

"That's because she's so small and flat," I said. "What we really need is a sloop with a protective cuddy that would block the spray."

"That would be nice," she said.

"What we need is a sloop that will slice through the water instead of pounding the way this one does all the time. We need a sloop with a deep cockpit and a broad beam. We need a boat with a lead keel and a permanent rudder and an inboard tiller. We need winches and sheaves and Egyptian cloth in our sails. We need . . ." I was so carried away by my endless list of specifications

96

that I took the wave from a passing yacht broadside. A wall of water washed across the deck, thoroughly drenching Sara but missing me. She let out a howl, "Watch what you're doing. What kind of a sailor are you, anyhow!"

The situation was to worsen considerably.

When we rounded Captree Island and headed toward the inlet, we found ourselves beating into a brisk wind. The whitecaps had formed; the waves slapped against our bow and doused us both. This was a new experience for me, for I was used to the shoal bay chop, but in the inlet the waves were swells and I could sense the depth of the sea. Sara blanched with each rise and fall of the tiny sloop, and the farther we sailed the paler she became.

The incoming tide funneled past Democrat Point, swirling in vicious eddies around red nuns and black cans, so that these channel markers seemed to be in motion too. Soon I realized our own forward thrust was more apparent than real. We couldn't buck the tide, and the boat was bobbing up and down faster than it was moving ahead. Sara began to moan.

"Look, Sara," I said, "we've got to come about and sail back to the Lighthouse dock. Sooner or later Ed is bound to come along and find us there."

"Yes, yes," Sara said, "do that, do!"

It took me three tries to bring the bow across the wind. Finally, with the wind astern, we skimmed along and came up to the Coast Guard dock beside the Lighthouse with no trouble. I secured the sloop and as soon as we stepped on the pier Sara felt better, and so did I. I was amazed at how frightened I was, for up to that moment

I had never ventured in a sailboat beyond the sheltered bay. But out here, near the inlet, I felt the unspent energy of the open sea that lured and scared me at the same time.

As we stood on the dock, I could see the broad expanse of the bay, a seething mass of whitecaps, from the inlet to Point O'Woods, from the Lighthouse to Bay Shore. I was struck by its breadth, and I saw that I still had a vast world to explore. I yearned to sail every channel, every creek. After I had exhausted the Great South Bay, I could log the miles eastward into Moriches Bay, then into Shinnecock Bay, then into Peconic Bay where Shelter Island squats between Long Island's two eastern prongs. But I would need something more substantial than a converted duckboat for that.

While these thoughts were passing through my mind, I saw two boats, almost at the same time. To the west I saw *Jove* bearing down the channel; to the north I saw the blue sloop approaching the Lighthouse in a sweeping arc. She was steeply heeled and her sails were close-hauled and stiff, her sharp prow knifing through the water, raising a foamy wake on either side. She beat to windward with surging power. The wind that had stymied me was made for her.

She came about within twenty yards of the dock and then eased off on a reach, with the wind across her starboard side. As she glided past, her standing helmsman trimmed the main sheet hand over hand and pushed the tiller to windward with his leg, ducking under the boom. The sloop jibed easily, showing her bright decks as she sailed away.

"What a beautiful boat," Sara said. "That's the most beautiful boat I've ever seen."

"She's a Timber Point," I said, "one of a couple dozen built two decades ago. She was the third one built, you can tell that by the number on her sail. But she's been rebuilt recently."

"How do you know that?"

"I know," I said. "I've seen her many times. I've asked around. The original Timber Points didn't have a cuddy and they didn't have bright decks. What's more, they had short masts and long booms while she has a tall mast and a short boom. So she has been re-rigged too."

"She's magnificent," Sara murmured, and I knew what was going through her mind. She was thinking how lovely it would be to moor a sloop like that in the Brightwaters Canal and point her out to friends. But, at that moment, showing off the blue sloop was the last thing on my mind. I wasn't thinking about her respectability; I was thinking about the latent power in her sails. I was thinking about the feel of the tiller in my hands. In such a sloop I could buck the tide; I could sail broad reaches across the bay; I could cruise alone for hours on end with no earthly concern except the breeze.

Ed eased *Jove* against the dock and I tied the duckboat to her stern.

"What happened?" he asked.

"The current was too strong," I said. "We had to turn around."

"You used your head," he said. "That was the thing to do."

I could see that he was pleased, and because he was pleased, I was pleased too.

Jove plowed against the current, towing the duckboat and a snub-nosed rowboat in tandem. As we neared the inlet, the tide slackened and gradually turned. By the time we anchored off Democrat Point, the bay was flowing a tortuous path past sand bars into the sea. In mid-channel, the water boiled and frothed, churned by wind and tide that clashed head-on. But Ed had found a quiet anchorage, protected from the warring elements by a spit of sand and windswept dunes.

I pulled the rowboat alongside and rowed the passengers ashore, two at a time: first Josie and Evelyn, then Aunt Flo and Uncle Bert.

Uncle Bert, who had bought the rowboat as a tender for *Jove*, wore a life preserver and clung to his seat until his knuckles turned white. It seemed strange to me that he should pay so dearly for something that scared him half to death. But when he realized the rowboat would let us explore otherwise inaccessible shores, he insisted on purchasing it. "If we have to have it, then we have to have it," he said with finality, a touch of fatalism in his voice. He was relieved, however, when we scraped bottom and he set foot on the beach.

When I rowed back to *Jove*, Sara climbed into the tender, expecting Ed to follow. Instead he handed her several buckets and basins from *Jove*'s galley, then he dove into the water and swam to shore. He propelled himself sidestroke, which seemed to suit his shortened arm, moving crablike toward the land. Sara seemed upset, for she was apparently expecting Ed to join her in the tender and all she had instead was a collection of disreputable pots and pails.

When Ed reached the beach, he strolled along the littoral where the withdrawing tide had exposed the sand, washing it smooth and clean. Suddenly he dropped to his knees and inspected a tiny hole. The water was dripping through his hair and glistening in the gray stubble on his face. We gathered around him and stared at the hole too, for he was our core, the center of our universe, and there was no telling what he would do next. Indeed, I doubted if he knew himself; like the wind, he seemed to move from some inner volition that was never entirely predictable. Yet at day's end all his unexpected acts seemed to add up, as if they had been preordained.

With his forefinger he drew a tight circle around the hole, which might have been bored by a sand worm. Then he dug carefully along the circumference, slowly raising his hands under the object, exposing its soft shell as if it were a precious jewel, satisfied that he had found what he was searching for. "Clams!" he said. "Don't stick your nose too close or you'll get a squirt of clam juice in your face."

It had to be if he said so. All that afternoon I watched for the sign of the spouting clam, but I never actually saw one that squirted straight up in the air.

Following Ed's example, we all searched for the small bores in the damp sand. We dug until our backs ached—strung out across the beach while the summer sun inched across the sky. Sometimes I would plunge into the water to cool off, then return to dig some more. Common terns dove for minnows off the shoals;

herring gulls camped along the slopes of the distant dunes, hoping (I imagined) that we might leave behind a minor feast. They hoped in vain.

"Won't they be sandy?" Aunt Flo asked.

"Not if we give them a chance to rinse themselves," Ed said.

As we dug the clams from their beds, Uncle Bert collected them and placed them in tepid pools so they could expel their grains of sand. By late afternoon we had dug several hundred. By my own estimate, I ate half of them myself during the following week and never once came upon a grain of sand.

Evelyn kept up a constant lament. "Oh, Ed, help me, I broke a shell! Oh, Ed, I cut my finger. Oh Ed, I can't dig anymore, my back hurts so!"

Sara and I converged on the same clam hole. "I wish she would shut up," Sara said. "She gives me a big swift pain!"

But Sara seemed to be the only one annoyed by Evelyn's complaints. Everyone else managed to ignore her.

Aunt Flo and Josie would dig a while, then pause and chat about sewing and school teaching, then dig some more. Uncle Bert was tending the clams like a little boy, making sure they cleansed themselves properly.

As for Ed, he had disappeared down the beach where he had seen two fishermen squatting in the sand, their long surf rods protruding from sand spikes. Soon thereafter he came back through the haze carrying a half-dozen blowfish in a pail and muttering a new word to me: "bouillabaisse." The events of the day were merging, as they always did when he was around. "Fishermen always leave blowfish behind," he said to me. "That's too

102

bad. They wouldn't do it if they knew how good they tasted."

I looked at the prickly skin on the bloated fish and thought of Gwen and her eels. They too had seemed repulsive at first, but the art was in extracting their essence, in knowing where the tender meat lay. In the case of blowfish, it was in their tails.

We left Democrat Point late in the afternoon and headed for Captree Island, where Ed knew a deserted cove. I steered *Jove* while he cleaned the fish, tossing the entrails overboard for the following gulls. Besides the blowfish, we also had bluefish, weakfish and a doormat fluke, all of which had been caught earlier in the day while Sara and I sailed.

In *Jove*'s galley, Ed sauted onion and garlic in olive oil until they were transparent, and then he dumped the mixture into an earthenware pot. Next he added a can of tomatoes, chopped parsley, lemon slices and even bay leaf, which he had on board. Then he put in his fish, and on top of the fish he dumped a mess of the steamer clams. When Aunt Flo wasn't looking, he furtively added a cup of white wine. "She'll never know the difference," he whispered to me. Finally he covered the whole business with a couple of inches of strained fish stock, which he had obtained by boiling the heads, bones and trimmings of the gutted fish. He clamped the lid on tight, stuck a board under the pot handle so two people could carry it through the soft sand, one on each side.

We moored on the lee side of Captree Island and walked over the sand dunes to the shore that faced the sea. Besides ourselves, there wasn't another soul on the abandoned beach. We gathered driftwood and heaped it

103

against a dune. The sun set over the inlet and a chill came into the air; the fire sizzled and popped and scorched the sand. The flames leaped and cut a jagged pattern against the darkening sky. Ed rigged a makeshift tripod and suspended the kettle over the embers as the flame died.

"It would be even better," he said, "if we had other kinds of fish. Sea robbin adds considerable flavor. So does a dash of squid. I was hoping we might hook a dogfish or catfish, also. Nothing like a little dogfish to liven up a stew."

"How about octopuses?" I said.

"Octopi," he said. "Very good. Also skate wings and goosefish tails."

He said he mixed his bouillabaisse from whatever fish he found at hand, and he had never made two fish stews that tasted the same. But even more enticing than the taste was the aroma, which mingled with the sea air and embraced us all—except for Sara, who was possessed by a deepening hunger that no amount of bouillabaisse could satisfy. I didn't understand Sara or the loneliness and envy that were consuming her.

"What's the matter, Sara? What's the matter with you?" I wanted to ask. But I kept my peace, pretending not to notice her black mood, and savored my fish stew. It warmed me. I stretched my body near the coals. The lighthouse beacon swung across the sky. I could see the flicker of lights from houses at a distant beach community under a sliver of moon.

Josie started to sing in a rich contralto, and Aunt Flo started to sing too. Then Uncle Bert began to sing, somewhat self-consciously, and so did Evelyn. Ed joined in, low and off-key, and everyone began to laugh, especially

Josie who knew he had sipped a little of the wine while making his fish stew.

Ed took Josie's hand and they walked along the beach, the gentle waves lapping against their bare feet. I could see their silhouette against the water, their disappearing footprints in the sand.

It was a late October day when I saw my duckboat for the last time. The air was crisp and white fluffs of cloud whipped across the sky. The wind gusted from the northwest, died out and gusted again. When it blew, the air was chill, but when it waned I could feel the warmth of the autumn sun through my clothes. I dismasted the sloop and carried the spars and rigging to their storage place under the Gowan house. I was about to drag the duckboat up the short beach into the reeds when I heard the screen door slam. Gwen stood on the deck for a moment, then leaned against the rail and called, "Rick, Daddy says to leave the boat in the water!"

I was startled by her appearance and I was trying to think of something ordinary to say. Finally a few innocuous words popped into my mind:

"Does he plan to do some shooting?" I said.

"No, but he doesn't want the boards to shrink up until after the hunting season ends."

I thought, "She's delivered her message and now she'll go inside." But I was wrong. She ambled toward the dock and sat on a post about twenty feet away from me. She was wearing a bulky knit sweater and shorts. Despite the biting wind, her legs and feet were bare. Her hair was pulled back and tied behind her head in a way that seemed to emphasize the strong lines of her face and the brightness of her eyes. She was a sturdy girl with solid legs and arms—yet, with it all, distinctly feminine.

I thrust my hands into my pockets, not because they were cold but because they suddenly felt awkward dangling by my side. I stared at the boat. "She looks so different without her spars," I said.

"Yes, she does."

I could feel Gwen's eyes move from me to the boat and back to me again. I sat on a post at the end of the dock, the deep water at my back. The north wind blew between us and then paused again. "She seems different than last time," I thought to myself. "More anxious, less sure."

"I hate the winter," I said.

"Do you?" she said. "Why?"

"Because I can't sail when it's so cold."

"You could join the Frostbite Club. They hold regattas all winter long."

It struck me as a typical thing for her to say. Eighty degrees or thirty degrees—it was all the same to her.

"No, I don't have a frostbite dinghy," I said. "Besides, cold weather sailing doesn't appeal to me. I like the sun and the warm wind."

She didn't respond.

"Do you like the winter?" I asked.

"I like it all right," she said. "It's not so bad."

"What do you like about the winter, anyhow?"

"I like the football games," she said. She went to Babylon High School, one town west of Bay Shore. It occurred to me that we might meet, even by accident,

106

when the two schools played. "Do you like football games?"

"No," I said, "I don't like football games."

"Then there are basketball games. You must like basketball."

"No, I don't care much for basketball, either."

"And the dances. The dances are fun." She did a little jig on the end of the dock, snapping her fingers.

"I don't dance," I said. "At least not well. Dancing seems sort of silly, anyhow."

"Well," she said, "you don't like football and you don't like basketball and you don't like to dance. What do you like, anyhow?"

"I told you," I said. "I like to sail."

"Sail, sail, sail," she said. "You can't spend your whole life sailing, you know."

"I'm sure going to try."

"Migosh!" she said, suddenly pointing toward the center of the channel. "Did you see that fish jump out there."

It seemed to me highly unlikely that fish would be jumping in the estuary in late October, but with Gwen around nothing about the inhabitants of the deep surprised me anymore. If she said she saw a fish jumping, then she must have seen a fish jumping.

She came alongside me, and I was only conscious of her nearness and the effect it had on me. She pointed toward the middle of the channel. "See!" she said. "Way out there! You can still see the ripples!"

I leaned forward, looking toward the distant spot, and the next thing I knew I was sailing through the air. I landed ten feet from the dock and dropped through the cold water like a stone. I surfaced before I realized I was saturated, and I climbed the ladder at the end of the dock before I knew for sure that Gwen had shoved me overboard. When I looked for her, I saw that she had retreated to the safety of the deck in front of her house.

I stood there doltishly, dripping, my shoes filled with water. "What's the big idea! What did you do that for?"

"I did it," she said, "because you're such a stuffed shirt. You're the biggest stuffed shirt I ever saw!"

It was perverse of me to tell Gwen I didn't like football or basketball. When I was in her presence the words I spoke seemed to run against the grain of what I felt. It was as if I were compelled to protect myself from what I wanted most. And what I wanted most was another chance—to return to the womb of the deserted dory and start all over again.

"Next time," I kept telling myself, "I won't let the opportunity slip away. Next time I'll reach out and touch her."

But when "next time" actually arrived, I was paralyzed by the same old dread. Instead of reaching out, I brushed her aside. I let her think I had no desire to see her once the summer came to an end.

Did she know? Did she care? I think she did, for she had the intuitive knowledge of the angler who senses the turbulence under the surface calm.

Besides, I saw her anyhow. As soon as I was old enough I played on the high school athletic teams. I saw her when Bay Shore played at Babylon and Babylon played at Bay Shore. I watched for her after games; our eyes would meet across the gym and we would drift toward each other and chat amiably—that much emotion I could afford.

And yet I was put off by the change that came over her, for Gwen wasn't the same girl in winter that she was in summer. Standing on the dock before her Oak Island summer home, she was loose and spirited as the wind, but in the high school gym, mingling with friends after a basketball game, her naturalness vanished and she glanced about anxiously to see if this or that boy were watching her. She wore mascara, and that bothered me; I felt as if her painted face came between us, transformed her into someone I didn't know. I began to yearn for the old Gwen, the girl in the white halter and tight shorts with an eel dangling at the end of her fishing line. Where had she gone?

Then one Friday night after a game, I saw her talking animatedly with two boys near the trophy room. She was blinking her lashes, throwing her head back as she laughed, and tossing her hair. I'd been cornered by some harebrained cheerleader who was reliving a critical moment of the game we'd just won. She couldn't seem to understand that the contest was already ancient history and my thoughts were elsewhere. Finally, distraught, I broke away and stalked across the gym. I grabbed Gwen by the arm and said, "Can I have a word with you?"

"What's the matter?"

"Nothing. I'd just like to have a word with you."

"Can't it wait?"

I gave her arm a yank and dragged her through the trophy room. I pulled her through a set of swinging doors into the crisp night air. The stars were bright and I could see her ghastly visage, with all its make-up, under the yellow light of the moon. I took a handkerchief from my pocket and began to wipe the junk from around her eyes.

"What are you doing?"

She struggled. I threw a free arm around her neck to hold her still. "I'm not going to let you do this to yourself," I said. "It's not you, Gwen, it's not you!"

She writhed, kicked my shins and then began to sob, the tears streaming down her cheeks. I let her go. Her face, streaked with mascara, appeared more hideous than before.

"I'm going to wipe that stuff off your face," I said, "if it's the last thing I do!"

I moved toward her again, carefully watching her right hand because I knew she could deliver a powerful blow. But it was her unseen left, a rising roundhouse from her knees, that caught me squarely on the jaw. I was lucky she struck me with her open hand and not her fist. The fresh slap echoed across the wintry sky, and when my head cleared I heard her crying as she raced for the safety of the gym. In an instant I was after her, but by the time I entered the school building she had disappeared.

I found a girl by the name of Margery Hubbard, whom I liked, and began to chat with her, as if nothing had happened. Gwen came out of the girl's room, her face washed and her eyes red. She was surrounded by a group of her friends who kept shooting dark glances my way. I felt a surge of masculine triumph, far more potent than any produced on the floor that evening. But my victory was short-lived, for the next time I saw Gwen she had defiantly painted her face again and appeared more frightful than before.

The heck with her I thought.

I began to dream about other girls, to devise fantasies and live them out in the elusive regions of my imagination. It was so much easier to dream about girls than contend with them in the flesh. In that way I wasn't subject to their whims; I was always in control. I made liaisons, broke them off, then made new ones without ever touching a real live girl.

I found only one way to ward off these obsessions, and that was to play as vigorously as I could, to lose myself in the spirit of the contest. The game became a compulsion, a momentary escape, that left me more frustrated than before.

In those days Bay Shore High School wasn't especially large, and the athletic coaches recruited any boy who showed better than average coordination in gym class. There are a large number of foolish notions about high school athletics around which parents, guardians, teachers and coaches rally, even though they know they aren't true. They all say, for example, that competitive sports mold boys, shape them into men. But deep down they know the athletic contest fulfills some atavistic urge to triumph that the human animal hasn't yet outgrown. They also say that athletics are a "good outlet" without ever specifying exactly what they mean. What they mean, of course, is that athletics allow otherwise excited young boys to let off steam.

None of these moralisms applied to me or to any other boy I knew. I learned very little about manhood from athletics, and my natural safety valve popped off with regularity, in spite of all the excess energy I channeled into sports. Why then did I play? I played partly because my coaches and my peers expected me to (not to play was to reveal some irreparable defect of character), but mostly to while away the winter days until the weather turned warm enough to set my sails. By the time I graduated high school, I had earned three varsity letters in football, two in basketball, and three in baseball. It was a long ordeal.

Of the three sports I played, I disliked football the most. I abhorred the roughness, the bone-smashing contact, the endless blocking and tackling, the cumbersome padding. But more than anything else I hated the trumped up zeal:

"Atta boy, Turk!"

"Great block, Beans!"

"Knock him over, Ding!"

Who needed it, anyhow.

Our coach, a spartan drillmaster who constantly urged us to "Talk it up! Talk it up!" switched me from quarterback to right end very early in my career because I lacked the spark to ignite a team. I had my moment of glory, even so. One Saturday afternoon, in the early minutes of a crucial game, the coach sent in a special pass play via a substitute.

"Seventy-six—to the right end," the sub announced.

"Oh no, that's me!" I muttered.

I raced downfield at the snap of the ball, faked to the right, faked to the left, then zipped around the defensive

112

back, a burly fellow twice my size. When I looked back over my shoulder, the football was spiralling over his outstretched fingertips. I stretched toward it; the ball bounced upward off my palms, and then I caught it on the rebound and tucked it into my arms. As I sprinted across the goal line, I glanced to my right and there, on the far side of the snow fence, Uncle Bert was dancing up and down amid the partisan spectators. For days afterward he told everyone he met: "That was my boy who caught that touchdown pass! Did you see him catch that pass? Did you ever see anyone run so fast?" What Uncle Bert didn't know was that I ran so fast because I was scared to death of being tackled from behind.

I looked forward to baseball, but there were only a few weeks late in May and early in June when it was warm enough to play. As soon as the sun climbed sufficiently high in the spring sky to warm the diamond, the high school season came to an abrupt end. I spent most of this season shivering around third base, hoping somebody would hit a ground ball my way, just for the exercise.

One early April day I was taking batting practice during a snow flurry. My fingers were stiff and the bat stung every time I hit the ball. Nevertheless I was determined to take my turn. I dug in at the plate; the coach hurled the ball and it sailed straight at my head. I saw it coming but I was too frozen to move. The ball struck my left ear. When I regained consciousness, a friend, who had been playing centerfield, was peering down at me with mild disinterest, asking if I was all right.

The coach drove me home and told Aunt Flo to take me to the doctor and have me checked for concussion, just in case. "The school insurance will pay for it," he explained, sensing her hesitancy. But for Aunt Flo this was one issue that transcended money. Doctors, like cigarettes and alcohol, were taboo. "There's no such thing as a personal injury," she told me, "in God's perfect world," and she read me long passages from *Science and Health* to prove her point.

My teammates thought otherwise; they told me that if I didn't see a doctor I would grow a cauliflower ear. Sara was so put off by my mangled ear that she wouldn't be seen in public with me until it healed.

Of all the sports, I found basketball the most enjoyable. The action was continuous and the physical contact minimal. A deliberately thrown elbow in those days was a rarity, especially in high school. The season was long and the game was played indoors where the weather was always predictable. The skimpy uniforms liberated arms and legs, and we had a new gym with an enormous court that permitted the players freedom and flexibility. I loved to run up and back until the sweat poured from my body and I was ready to drop.

The junior varsity squad, on which I played as a freshman and sophomore, practiced after the varsity, which meant it was dark before I began my long trek home. One evening after practice I realized I had forgotten a book in my school locker. I left the gym, after showering and dressing, and jogged along a dark corridor, barely able to see more than a few feet ahead of me as I ran. Suddenly I heard the shattering of glass, and I reeled as though struck by a blow. Gradually I came to my senses and realized I had crashed into the glass door of the music room. Dazed, I stepped into the cold night air and felt the deep stinging, as though a lash of a thousand nettles had whipped my face. Under a street lamp, I saw the red stains on my clothes. I ran in terror, but not toward home.

It was nearly two miles to Ed's house. Josie answered the door and nearly fainted when she saw the bloody spectre standing before her.

"Ed! Ed!" she shrieked.

Ed took me into the kitchen, poured warm water into a basin and washed my face. "You're lucky," he said, "it missed your eyes. There doesn't seem to be any glass in the cuts, but you've got quite a gash on your nose. We'll have to take you to a doctor for that."

"Aunt Flo won't be pleased," I said.

"To heck with Aunt Flo!" he said.

The doctor put three stitches in my nose and applied antiseptic to all the lacerations. Then he gave Ed a prescription for a drug to calm me down.

We went back to Ed's house where I stretched out on the couch and took the pill with a small glass of buttered rum. I was shivering under a comforter, but I soon felt the warmth from the roaring fire across the room. Ed and Josie were sitting opposite me, shoeless, warming their toes.

They started to laugh.

"Fool kid," Ed said to me. "What's the idea of running along a dark corridor, anyhow?"

I wanted to laugh too, but when I opened my mouth I could feel the cuts on my face and the stitches in my nose.

"It was pretty dumb," I managed to say.

"Is there anything you'd like?" Josie asked.

"How about playing 'Hindustan,' " I said.

She put the record on the victrola while Ed went into another room to call Aunt Flo. I don't know what he told her; I imagine she was relieved that Ed had taken this burden off her hands. I was asleep before he returned. In my dream I saw Ed and Josie whirling around the floor. Then I saw my own parents emerge from the sparks in the fire and dance across the room. My father, straight-backed and dashing, was looking down at my mother, and my mother had her left arm around his neck. Her head was thrown back and her eyes were bright and laughing.

One Saturday morning, closeted in my bedroom under the eaves, I read a heartsick poem by Stephen Vincent Benet, which he apparently wrote while living in Europe and pining for his native land,

> *I have fallen in love with American names,*
> *The sharp names that never get fat,*
> *The snakeskin-titles of mining-claims,*
> *The plumed war-bonnet of Medicine Hat,*
> *Tucson and Deadwood and Lost Mule Flat . . . .*

I read that poem over and over again until I had it memorized. As I recited the words under my breath, I pictured scenes that those place-names conjured up, and I felt the patriotism that comes to a man when he senses not the power but the abiding peace of the land where he was born. Even those places I had never seen except in photographs—"Harrisburg, Spartanburg, Painted Post"—aroused within me an indefinable yearning akin to wanderlust. In the quiet of my secluded room I lay on my bed, glanced through the window at the barelimbed trees and tried to quell my restlessness.

Like the poet, I too had fallen in love with American names, but the names I cherished most—Hubbard, Mowbray, Brewster, Watts—bore the distinct Yankee stamp of trader ships and whaling days. I felt that the people who owned such names had centuries of salty history in their bones. Their ancestors had settled in and around Sag Harbor along the protected shores of Peconic Bay, and the visitor to that sea-faring hamlet can still find in a small museum there the harpoons and other relics they once used.

All through the ensuing decades Southards, Munceys, Ravens, Drakes and Doans scattered like seeds across Suffolk County. They founded local banks, shipyards, hardware stores and, eventually, the more prosperous insurance and real estate agencies. A few even made their way into high public office trading on their family names. Most had long since forsaken the sea for more lucrative landlocked trades, but a few clung to their heritage despite the economic sacrifice, for by the twentieth century it was exceedingly difficult for them to make a decent living from their boats.

I especially admired Schuyler Hubbard, the charter boat captain who lived a few doors down from Ed Doubrava, closer to the bay. I learned from Captain Hubbard's youngest daughter, Margery, that he was once one of the ablest sailors on the bay. He raced Islip One-Designs—sleek, shoal-drafted, gaff-rigged sloops, that had all but disappeared from the Great South Bay by the time I learned to sail.

In his earlier years, Margery told me, her father ran a large open-party boat in which he took fishermen out into Fire Island Inlet for so much a head. Now he supported his family with his stubby converted Crosby catboat, *Nimrod*, which he chartered to families by the day. They came for a day's fishing aboard *Nimrod* from the horse country of Westbury and the far reaches of Central Park West.

Margery told remarkable stories about her father—how, for example, he taught her to row by setting her adrift in a dory in the creek behind her house. The huge, two-tiered Ocean Beach ferry bore down on her while her father, the Captain, laughed uproariously on the dock and thumped his thigh. I suspected she wasn't as far adrift as she suspected and he was standing ready with a long boat hook to fetch her back.

The mere thought of Margery Hubbard helplessly asea sent a shiver of pleasure along my spine. I imagined Margery drifting not down the creek behind her house but through the treacherous inlet toward the open ocean. I could see her plainly, huddled in the rowboat, frightened and cold. Then I saw myself braving the elements, sailing out to rescue her from certain death.

Margery's vision of me, however, was somewhat less heroic. She had a notion that I would make a first-rate class president.

"Margery," I said, "I don't want to be president. I'm not cut out for that sort of thing."

"Sure you are," she said. "You'll make a fine president. We need somebody dependable like you."

She was so ingenuous I found it impossible to resist. If Margery said I could be president, then I could be president; if she said I could shake the earth, then I could shake the earth. I don't know whether I was honored more by my election or knowing that Margery Hubbard supported me.

Everyone believed in Margery Hubbard; if she said I could do the job who would dare say otherwise! Yet Margery Hubbard would have been appalled to discover the passions she aroused in me.

Whenever I stayed overnight at Ed Doubrava's house, which I often did, I would find myself strolling past the Hubbard house in the dark. I would step into the chill night air and find Orion's belt studded against the wintry sky. Then I would locate the entire, stolid figure of the intrepid hunter, his feet planted firmly amid the stars. He was a giant, even among gods, Orion was. Emboldened by his presence, I would stroll past the doll house in which the Hubbards lived, gaze up at Margery's second-story bedroom window and imagine all sorts of improbable things.

Yet, despite my obsession, I never took the pains to find out who Margery Hubbard really was. I knew she had a face bred out of Peregrine White and Virginia Dare, but I had no idea what she liked and what she despised. Unlike Gwen she wasn't flesh and blood, someone who was unpredictable or threatened me with a dangling eel. Like Orion, she was a myth, a cluster of notions no closer than a constellation faintly traced against the sky. She was sweet, thoughtful, unpretentious Margery Hubbard—but most of all, a Hubbard, a mythic piece of America:

> *I will remember Carquinez Straits,*
> *Little French Lick and Lundy's Lane*
> *The Yankee ships and the Yankee dates*

120

And the bullet-towns of Calamity Jane
I will remember Skunktown Plain . . . .

And at that time of my life I found it safer to fall in love with a myth than with a girl who actually lived and breathed.

When I told Aunt Flo about my election, she was mystified. She sat me down at the kitchen table and inquired into all the details, and then she made a cryptic statement that puzzled me for a long time. "Sara has all the aces," she said, "but you're taking in all the cards."

I thought she meant that Sara had the advantage of natural parents while I had to make my own way, cut off from my birthright, so to speak. But it seemed to me, even then, that a child is often better off having no parents than the wrong parents, for if a child has the wrong parents there is no escape and the entrapment lasts a lifetime. With no parents he can pick and choose his models from the world at large.

That was the main advantage I had over Sara, growing up. If my detachment was my cross, it was also my saving grace. I didn't need to accept Sara's parents as my own, but Sara had no choice. She had to test them constantly to see if she still had their affection and esteem. Of course, that was something I didn't realize at the time. I was so preoccupied with myself that I didn't think about the traumatic effect my sudden appearance must have had on Sara's life. Before my arrival, she was the ornamental centerpiece; but after I materialized she had to worry that I might display a distracting luster of my own.

Aunt Flo and Uncle Bert had vowed to treat Sara and me as equals, and they did to the extent their bias allowed. But when it came to accomplishments, they constantly made invidious comparisons between their daughter and their nephew. Thus they intimated that Sara was quick and bright and I was slow and dull. Sara was nimble and I was awkward. Sara had an ear for music and could draw pleasant pictures while I was tone deaf and couldn't draw a straight line, even though I was the son of an artist. For a long time I felt as if any aptitude I showed was contrary to nature.

Yet these comparisons hurt Sara more than me, for my little successes surprised her and she couldn't accept them when they came. When she heard about my election, she said flippantly: "Class president is a silly position, anyhow. Everybody knows the students always pick the biggest clown." Aunt Flo, to her discredit, laughed at Sara's appraisal as though she concurred, even though I knew from her earlier statements about Sara's aces and my cards that she felt differently.

Sara didn't know about her mother's disparaging remark, for I never repeated it to her, although I was sorely tempted to, especially when we performed our sing-song skit "For One Has To Be Careful, Hasn't One?"

In those days a percentage of the money Aunt Flo earned in her dressmaking business was invested in dancing and dramatic lessons for Sara and, for a time, in me. Other than the fact that I learned to tap a waltz clog to "Sweet Rosie O'Grady," the money was squandered on my account. But Aunt Flo was persuaded that Sara was destined for stardom. After all, the Crisp sisters,

122

who gave dancing and dramatic lessons in their rented house and who had connections in Hollywood, told her so.

Winnie Crisp was in charge of the dance school. She was a scarecrow of a woman with buck teeth and long blond hair that she wore in braids halfway down her back, and who had earned a reputation on the London stage for toe dancing in her bare feet. Dora Crisp was in charge of the dramatic school. Her hair was cut boyishly short in black and lay in bangs across her forehead, a severe style that matched her scowl. When Sara sang, Dora would nod approvingly, but she couldn't understand why I couldn't hit Middle C after she banged it out a half-dozen times in a row on her straightback piano.

It was all so ludicrous. I knew I was off-key and I also knew there was nothing I could do about it. But Dora Crisp was convinced that I could hit the right note by rote. All she had to do was repeat Middle C often enough and the sound would become indelibly imprinted in my mind. She split my skull with Middle C but my voice still refused to duplicate the sound.

Dora Crisp was a drillmaster, and she made Sara and me rehearse "For One Has To Be Careful, Hasn't One?" over and over again.

The skit was built on a familiar plot: Boy meets Girl, Girl rebuffs Boy, Boy pursues Girl, Girl slaps Boy, Boy puts his hand to red face and says: "For One Has To Be Careful, Hasn't One?" whereupon the audience laughs and says of the Girl: "Isn't she adorable!" as the Boy skulks off the stage. One day Sara delivered her climactic slap with such deliberate force that my teeth rattled. I was set back and dazed. As we walked home along Main

123

Street from the Crisp sisters' house, I said, "You did that on purpose."

"Did what on purpose?"

"Slapped me that hard."

"Oh, don't be such a crybaby. The slap has to be realistic, so you might as well get used to it."

"Well, I've got news for you. I'm not going to get used to it. What's more, you're going to have to find a new face to slap."

"What do you mean?"

"Just that. I'm going to tell your mother I don't want to have anything to do with the Crisp sisters and their stupid dance studio any more."

"She won't let you stop."

"Oh yes she will. She'll figure out how much money she can save and then she'll say: 'All right, Rick, that's all right, just as long as you know that anything we provide for Sara we provide for you.' And then I'll say . . ."

"Shut up!"

"What?"

"Shut up, I said."

I was furious and she knew it, and now she was looking for a way to get back at me. She then said, "Why do you go over there all the time, anyhow?"

"Where?"

"You know where I mean."

I knew she meant Ed's house, and I was afraid she knew I was walking up and down the deserted street past Margery's house at night. She knew I liked Margery and she constantly urged me to call her, but I didn't have the courage to pick up the phone.

124

"I go there because I go there," I replied.

"Well, you shouldn't go there so much. How do you know they want you hanging around?"

"If they didn't want me hanging around, they would say so, wouldn't they?"

"Besides, Mommy and Daddy are getting suspicious."

"Suspicious of what?"

"You know."

"No, I don't." She had a maddening way of implying things, of drawing information from me I didn't want to reveal.

"Of Josie and Evelyn."

"What about them?"

"Mommy says they're Ed's concubines."

"His what!"

"Concubines. Look it up in the dictionary if you don't know what it means."

"I know what it means. I also know it's not true."

"You once told me you thought he liked both of them."

"I know I did. But I don't think so anymore."

"I think you're wrong and Mommy's right."

"Well, you're both wrong."

"How do you know?"

"Because I know. Ed wouldn't do anything like that."

"Do you snoop around trying to find out while you're over there?"

"Of course not!"

"Well, why do you go over there?"

Exasperated, I spoke a simple truth. "I go over there because I'm comfortable there." Sara and I had discussed the difference between Ed's house and our house many times, and I supposed she would understand. At Ed's house we could slump into a frayed couch, but at our house we were scared to sit down on a slipcovered chair for fear of crumpling the cushions. At Ed's house the fireplace was filled with pine and maple ashes, but at our house the fireplace was strictly ornamental because Aunt Flo objected to the way it spewed soot and smoke.

"Well," Sara said, "I don't plan to go to Ed's house anymore."

"Why not? Because you're afraid your mother will object?"

"No," she said. "Because I don't feel comfortable there, even if you do."

"You don't feel comfortable there?" I asked incredulously. I couldn't comprehend the spite that motivated her remark.

"You wouldn't understand," she said, turning her head away as though she were guarding a wound.

I grabbed her by the shoulders and turned her around. "What do you mean—I wouldn't understand?"

"Mommy doesn't want me hanging around a man like that."

"You're making that up! Your mother never said that!"

"No, she never said that, but I know that's the way she feels."

"Sara, what are you saying? What's going through your mind?"

"It's not my fault," she said. "I can't help the way he looks at me."

I felt as if I had been slapped again, except this time there was no physical blow—but something worse, an

126

immutable force over which I had no control. "Sara, I don't know what you're thinking, but whatever it is, you'd better be careful."

She glowered at me for a moment, then skipped backward along the sidewalk. "You'd better be careful! You'd better be careful!" she said, mimicking and taunting me at the same time. Then, in one of her rapier thrusts, she added: "For one has to be careful, hasn't one?" and danced beyond my reach.

During the early days of World War II, when building materials were still in supply, Uncle Bert and Ed built three houses on speculation and sold them readily at a tidy profit. They were modified two-story Capes that appeared lived-in even before they were occupied. Ed saw to the construction, Uncle Bert to the financing, and I to the sweeping up of sawdust when I wasn't in school, sailing or being hectored by Dora Crisp about my diction and about being tone deaf.

The two men were enthusiastic about their prospects; they would sit on *Jove*'s stern—Ed listening and nodding and Uncle Bert discoursing about "pent-up demand," unaware of the weakfish nibbling on his line. His mind was wandering amid the scores of custom Capes he and Ed would build someday along the south shore—fine homes of value that people would still be living in two centuries hence.

"Quick, Uncle Bert," I would yell, "set the hook!"

Uncle Bert would give his line a tremendous jerk. Sometimes he would split the delicate weakfish at its tender gills, and sometimes he would swing it clear through the air in a perfect arc until it landed flat on *Jove*'s canopy where it would flop haplessly about. Whenever that happened, Ed would laugh and tell Uncle Bert he had caught another one of those "flying fish." Then Ed would take the fish from the hook for Uncle Bert and bait the hook again, and Uncle Bert would drop his line over the stern and start to talk about pent-up demand once more.

"What's the matter with them anyhow!" Sara would complain to me. "All they talk about is buying land. They want to buy this parcel and look into that parcel. Who cares?"

But Aunt Flo felt differently. She would sit nearby in a deck chair, her face caressed by the breeze and tilted toward the sun, listening to the conversation and dreaming (I suspected) about the money the two men would make. "Can I get you some fruit juice, Aunt Flo?" I asked one time.

"It's a partnership made in heaven," she replied.

At about the same time Uncle Bert made some excellent business connections in New York and his small firm was involved in the title search and mortgage guarantee for the sale of several large commercial buildings in Brooklyn and Queens. Although these transactions were infrequent, they did improve the Mann household income—even Aunt Flo had to acknowledge that. To Sara's relief, she closed her dressmaking shop and announced that henceforth she would dedicate herself to her husband, which—to Aunt Flo—meant keeping house even more diligently than before.

One duty (she referred to all jobs as "duties") she took upon herself was the preparation of food for our weekends aboard *Jove*. Some women might go to the deli and stock up on cold cuts, potato salad and cole slaw, but not Aunt Flo. She insisted on making everything herself. Consequently, her food preparation duties began early Monday and continued all week. She worked herself into a frazzle getting ready to enjoy herself.

One day Sara went into the kitchen amid all her mother's demon preparations and began to complain about the inadequacies of "our little duckboat." I was appalled, for she couldn't have chosen a worse time to raise the subject. Aunt Flo was up to her armpits in mayonnaise for the potato salad; one cake she'd baked had nearly exploded and another had collapsed. In addition, she'd discovered that she had run out of brown sugar, and she was now sitting at the kitchen table, steeping a two-day-old tea bag in a cup of tepid water, trying to collect herself. This was the moment Sara picked to launch her campaign to get us a sloop of our very own.

"Don't bother me now about that!" Aunt Flo said.

I tried to ease Sara out of the kitchen but she kept elbowing me in the rib cage.

"But Mommy . . ."

"Not now, Sara!" Aunt Flo said again.

"But listen, Mommy . . ."

"Not now! Can you hear me! Not now!"

Sara stamped her foot. "You never listen to me! You never have time to listen to anything I say."

"What do you mean, you ungrateful child. Look at all the sacrifices I make for you!"

I saw all my hopes for acquiring a boat slipping away. And yet my sympathies at the moment were with poor, badgered Aunt Flo. Even though most of her suffering was self-inflicted, it still seemed to me undeserved. She couldn't help the fact that she paid no attention to Sara. She didn't mean it to be that way.

"Not now, Sara, not now," I muttered to no avail.

"What sacrifices?" Sara shouted. "You're always too busy to listen to me. Whenever I ask you something, you always say: 'Not now, Sara, not now!'"

With that, Aunt Flo went to her stove and dumped all the food she was cooking and all the cakes she was baking into the garbage pail.

"There," she said, "how do you like that! Now nobody's going out on Ed's boat. Nobody. It's a punishment."

By the time Uncle Bert came home, the maelstrom had abated, but for three days we all wondered if we would ever go out on *Jove* again. Uncle Bert rubbed his hands and waited for the storm to pass. As much as he wanted to go out on Ed's boat, he still wouldn't go down to the deli and buy the cold cuts and potato salad himself. But when Ed heard about Aunt Flo's pronouncement, he said, "Who's she punishing, anyhow?"

I think he meant she was punishing the one person she had vowed to help: Uncle Bert. But after a while I realized the only person Aunt Flo was punishing was herself, for she was the one who was most transformed whenever *Jove* pulled away from the dock. Fortunately, she seemed to realize that too. Eventually she came out from behind her locked bedroom door and began cooking and baking all over again, banging around the kitchen until all hours of the night to make up for lost time. But the moment she left the land all her tensions and antagonisms dissolved. She leaned back in her deck chair and listened to Uncle Bert tell Ed about all the money they would make when Hitler was dead and the terrible war came to an end.

Meanwhile, Sara persisted as only Sara could. She pouted, threatened, sulked, withdrew and attacked again. Ultimately, of course, she prevailed, but the victory came so easily that it hardly seemed to depend on all the anguish and travail.

One day Uncle Bert came home on an early train in an exuberant mood. He had just left an important "closing"—one of those real estate terms I heard constantly as a boy and never understood. I gathered, however, that "closings" were important events for Uncle Bert, for he always came home early after one and went down to Freistadts and devoured a sundae with two scoops of vanilla ice cream, as he did this day. After he finished his second scoop, he leaned back in the booth and said, "Well now, let's talk about that boat once more. I'll tell you what—I'll buy you a sailboat if you'll agree to two conditions." He glanced at Sara and then at me.

Conditions: they sounded ominous, but I was prepared to accept any terms even before I knew what they were. Besides, I could see that Uncle Bert was in a mellow mood. Ice cream sundaes had the same effect on Uncle Bert as whiskey on other men.

"First," he said, "it must be understood that the boat belongs to both of you. I don't want to hear any arguments about who is going to sail and who is going to stay home."

We assured him that this would be no problem—either we would both sail or both stay home. Secretly, I was counting on Sara tiring of the boat within a few weeks after the initial excitement of ownership wore off.

"Second," he said, "I won't spend more than three hundred dollars for the boat, including sails."

"Three hundred dollars," Sara said to me later when we were alone. "It's not an awful lot."

"Only a fortune," I replied.

"But it will never buy a boat like that blue one we saw."

"No, it won't do that. But it will buy something better than that duckboat we've been sailing around."

I was still uncertain, however, for Aunt Flo usually had the final word. But several days later she remarked in the middle of supper, "Sailing is such a lovely sport, and you children should be grateful that you have the opportunity."

For Aunt Flo, something was either a downright evil or an absolute good, and one paid for the good things with eternal gratitude.

But I also thought Aunt Flo had been favorably impressed that summer day we sailed the duckboat together along the lee shore. It was then she saw that sailing was as essential to me as swimming had once been to her. From that day on I detected a change in her attitude. I could disappear for hours, even overnight, and she never expressed the slightest qualm. When I was sailing she seemed to feel as though I were under the protection of a benign God, and so did I.

Every weekend for three months, Ed, Sara and I scouted the south shore shipyards from Bay Shore to Hampton Bays. I don't know of a better place to be than a shipyard as the winter wanes and the collected snow melts on the canvas covers and the ice cracks in the creeks. The boatmen mill aimlessly about, worrying the sun across the southern sky, wondering if it will ever start to climb. Then one day the warmth is there beyond the thaw and the bluebills, mergansers and buffleheads are gone. Shipyards in April are always muddy and always alive with anticipation, for the baymen know that at any moment the wind might turn. And when it does they will peel back their tarps along their temporary frames and expose their dark and moldy decks to the fresh wind from the sea.

In those days of wooden boats, hulls weren't cast from a common mold and it was still possible to find a variety of custom sloops over and above the one-design racing classes: Stars, Snipes, Comets, Lightnings and Cape Cods. I saw two boats I liked. One was a 16-foot gaff-rigged catboat built a half-century earlier by Crosby at Osterville on Cape Cod. She reminded me of the ubiquitous clamboats baymen constantly converted to power from sail: beamy, shoal-draft boats with spacious decks suitable for keeping one's balance while manipulating long rakes and tongs. In truth, I preferred a sloop to a catboat, but this one had indisputable character. I admired her broad transom and the way she flared amidships toward the bow. I admired her thick stem, which could split any wave. But Sara didn't share my enthusiasm. "She reminds me of the fat lady in the circus," she said.

The other was a 19-foot Lightning, a racing sloop prevalent on the bay, and as different from the catboat as any boat could be. The catboat spoke to sea-kindliness and patience; she was built for idling away a summer day. But the Lightning was sleek and cramped, designed for speed. Sara didn't like the Lightning either—there was something about the spartan appearance of this stripped-down racing sloop that put her off. She was made for beating to windward, not for show.

At last we found a sloop that didn't violate Sara's sense of aesthetics. She was a round-bottomed, 18-foot boat that had all the virtues of an oversized bathtub. But Sara judged a boat by its trim, and this boat had, besides mahogany coaming, two varnished mahogany cabinet doors that opened to a locker under the deck. Sara was so bedazzled by those mahogany doors she didn't see anything else. Ed expressed reservations about her rounded bottom. "She's sure to roll some," he said, but how much he didn't know, for she was high and dry on the ways at the shipyard in Bellport. He suggested that we wait until she was launched to make a final judgment, but Sara would have none of it. She had, in fact, disputed nearly everything he said since the search began, and he wasn't disposed to argue with her now. Since Sara was satisfied and since the price was right, we bought her and prayed she would prove to be more stable than she seemed. As I saw it, it was either this boat or no boat, for we had run out of shipyards.

"I told you I'd get Daddy to buy us a sailboat," Sara said, quite pleased with herself, as we drove home in Ed's car. "I told you that, didn't I?"

"Yes, you did, Sara. Yes you did."

"What shall we call her?"

"How about *O Boat!?*" I suggested. Her rounded bottom reminded me of the letter O sliced horizontally in half.

"Oh no!" Sara said, "that will never do." She thought

134

for a while, nibbling on her fingernails, and finally said: "*Lively Lady*—that's what we'll christen her!"

Her eyes brightened, as if she had a vision of herself smashing a champagne bottle against *Lively Lady*'s hull as she slid down the ways.

"What makes you think she'll be so lively?"

"Oh, she'll be lively, all right. Just you wait and see!"

Ed said he would tow *Lively Lady* from the shipyard, which was in Bellport, to her berth in the Brightwaters Canal on the first warm Saturday in May. "Just the three of us," he said. "We'll have a good time."

"It will be fun," I agreed, but Sara, sitting between Ed and myself in the front seat, stared straight ahead through the windshield without saying a word. "Don't you think it will be fun, Sara?" I inquired.

"How far is it?" she asked.

"About forty miles, round trip," Ed replied.

"Well," she said, "I only hope it doesn't take all day."

All day—that was the romance; it would take all day to sail to Bellport aboard *Jove* and tow *Lively Lady* home. I looked ahead to the event, but when I awoke on the appointed morning the dogwood was in bloom and the tree pollen in the air. I staggered to the bathroom, dampened a cloth with warm water and washed the heavy discharge from my itchy eyes. Then I sneezed ten times in a row, the spasms racking my body in violent waves, leaving my legs weak and my throat and nasal passages inflamed. I had no antihistamines, nothing to ward off my debilitating sneezing fits except a stack of large white handerchiefs that Aunt Flo boiled in vinegar at the end of each day. Aunt Flo was mortally afraid of vermin, and she reacted to my sneezing seizures as though I were filling the air with deadly germs.

I ate breakfast: orange juice, Wheaties with fresh strawberries and a hot cup of coffee to help shrink the sinus membranes. The strawberries raised white hot prickles on the roof of my mouth and I started sneezing again.

"I can't make it, Sara," I said, giving my red nose a vigorous blow. "I'll never make it to Bellport today."

I was disheartened. Here I had waited patiently for so long to acquire a sloop of my own, and now that the time had arrived to fetch her home I was too ill to leave the house. If the wind had been blowing on-shore, I might've attempted the trip, but there were puffy off-shore airs, and so the bay was no haven for a hayfever sufferer. My best course was to hole up in my bedroom under the eaves, lock the window, bolt the door and pray that the invisible enemy wouldn't invade the cracks between the walls.

Sara was neither sympathetic nor dismayed. "Don't worry," she said, "Ed and I can manage alone."

"If you don't mind," I said.

"Mind? Why should I mind?"

"I just thought . . ."

"Thought what?" she snapped.

"That you didn't like him."

"Well," she said, "it's just a short trip, and it is a lovely day." She headed for the garage door and at the last moment turned to say,

"Rick, I am sorry you can't come. But you'll be miserable if you do, and you've lots of good sailing days ahead."

I watched Uncle Bert back the car out of the driveway from my bedroom window. Then I lay back on my bed, handkerchief over my face, and thought of the sparkling bay. I saw *Jove* plying her way eastward against the rising sun, then heading home while the fiery ball was still high in the western sky. I saw Ed at the wheel, glancing back now and again to make sure *Lively Lady* was secure, and I saw Sara . . .

I didn't see Sara. I couldn't see her anywhere aboard *Jove*. My imagination wouldn't place her there.

It was late in the day when Sara finally returned, and I expected her to charge into my room. *"Lively Lady* is at her berth," she would say, "safe and sound! And she looks so pretty!" I waited, and when she didn't come I attributed it to her spitefulness. I went to my bedroom door and opened it tentatively.

"Sara," I called.

No answer—only the murmur of voices, or was it the radio?

"Sara," I called again, and then I heard the voices again, low and secretive, downstairs. "What's going on?"

"You stay in your room!" Aunt Flo called.

I shut the door firmly from the outside to make it sound as if I had obeyed. Their muffled voices travelled up the stairwell. Sara was speaking, her voice high and cracking, and Aunt Flo and Uncle Bert were pumping her with questions.

"Then what did he do?" Aunt Flo would ask.

"Then what did you do?" Uncle Bert would say.

After they had extracted the information they wanted, Aunt Flo said, "Now you go upstairs. Your father and I want to talk."

Sara came up to me.

"What happened?"

"We got the boat, that's what happened."

"Is that all?"

She pushed me into my room and closed the door.

"On the way home . . ." she began.

"On the way home . . . what?"

". . . he made an advance."

"Oh Sara, come on!" I gazed at her steadily, but she didn't drop her eyes. I had the feeling she was pleased with herself and would laugh in triumph if she thought I would approve.

"It's so, it's so," she said and nodded sadly as if to convey the terrible ordeal she had been through.

"You're lying!" I said.

Now her eyes blazed.

"You're making that up!" I said.

"I am not. How dare you!"

"Tell me what happened. I want to know every little detail."

"I'd rather not," she said, pulling back in feigned horror, as if the details were too sordid for my tender ears.

"Every word. Every detail. I have a right to know. He is my friend."

"Some friend! Some friend—that's all I have to say. You should pick your friends with greater care!"

"Sara!"

She moved toward the door and I leaped in her way. I had to restrain myself from striking her. I wanted to pummel her, knock her to the ground.

"All right," she said, "if you must know the gory details, here they are. He went down into the cabin. I didn't know what for. When he came back up on deck he had something in his hand."

138

"Sara, Sara," I groaned.

"Oh yes, he had something in his hand!"

"I mean what happened next. What did you say?" I asked, realizing I was now beginning to sound a little like Aunt Flo and Uncle Bert. But Sara had a tantalizing way of disclosing bits and pieces of information at a time.

"I didn't say anything. What could I say?"

"What did he do?"

"What did he do? Wasn't that enough!"

So that was it: Sodom and Gomorrah and the seduction of Lady Jane. I looked at Sara. She was now sixteen, a junior in high school, well-formed and physically attractive. It was possible that Ed was guilty of an indiscretion. Yet I knew Sara was capable of making it all up.

"You don't believe me," she said defiantly.

"I don't know," I said. "I just don't know." I felt it was foolish of him if he did it, and despicable of her to create a row.

I went to the head of the stairs again and I heard Uncle Bert dialing on the downstairs phone. His voice wavered but his manner was firm, as if he had steeled himself to perform a task he would rather have ignored. "She's just a little girl," he kept saying, "just a little girl! What do you want with a little girl?"

I turned toward that little girl. "Oh Sara, Sara," I said, "what have you done!"

When I went downstairs Uncle Bert was sitting in an armchair with his head buried in his hands. His unbuilt Capes had vanished, his partnership dissolved, and his happy summer weekends aboard *Jove* had come to a close. He looked up at me and said: "She's just a little girl! What did he want with a little girl?"

Sometime later I heard that Ed had sold his house on the creek and that he and Josie had moved further east on the Island where Ed built vacation homes. I also heard that he and Josie had finally married; but I never saw either of them again.

*S*ara *sailed with me all through the month of June. By*
July 4, she said she was sick of sailing and vowed never
to sail again—"especially in that tub." She retired to a
patch of sand on the Brightwaters beach and watched me
tack offshore, trying to maneuver the recalcitrant sloop.

Lively Lady had the grace of a hippopotamus. At her
berth she sat high in the water, exposing her copper red
bottom. Under sail, she rocked and rolled, even after I
had placed several hundred pounds of window sash-
weights in her bilge. She was sluggish in light airs and
stubborn in a spanking breeze. Her jib was miscut, her
turnbuckles frozen and her rudder too small.

"What a goshawful crate!" said Simm Wicks, one of
the hands at Anson's shipyard, as he tried to shift the
rake of her mast to eliminate her lee helm. The boat was
freakish; instead of heading up into the wind (as a well-
balanced boat should do) when I let go of the tiller, she
veered off and, on a broad reach, threatened to jibe.
"Don't you venture downwind on a blustery day, you
hear? You're liable to never get home. Of course, that

might be a blessing to your ma and pa, but I wouldn't care to see a handsome young man like you get drowned!"

Nearby, Wesley Wicks, Simms older brother, was flat on his back under the *Miss Ocean Beach*, caulking her seams. He let out a raspy laugh. "Why don't you let off twitting that young fella, Simmy," Wes said. "Can't you see he's got trouble enough without your gas!"

"I used to know a nice young man like you," Simmy went on as he fussed with the shrouds. "He had a real purpose in life too. He had set his sights on doing something useful, like running a ferry boat or a shipyard. Then one day his parents upped and bought him a sailboat that wouldn't behave herself no matter how many times he altered the rake of her mast. She wallowed about and had a lee helm just like yours. By the time that young man was eighteen he was a total cynic, all because of that mulish boat of his. Instead of growing up to be a worthwhile member of society, he went to college and became a lawyer instead."

Wes blared, his trumpet voice carrying across the small island in the creek that was Anson's shipyard.

Simm and Wes were leathery men in their early sixties. Both were separated from the Coast Guard. During Prohibition, they were responsible for tracking down rumrunners. But, instead of blocking their way, they were accused of letting the smugglers slip undetected through Fire Island Inlet with their contraband. One story said they had been dishonorably discharged, another that they had actually gone to prison. Now they eked out an existence at Anson's, scrubbing and painting the bottoms of those same rumrunners, lately converted

142

to ferries, like the swift, low-slung *Miss* that regularly split the bay with her steep wake.

Simmy, weather-beaten and squinty-eyed, lived at the boatyard aboard his 28-foot clamboat with her built-up trunk cabin that made her seem topheavy even though she skimmed up and down the busy creek with perfect aplomb. He had set up a small typewriter in the cabin and pecked away on it in his spare time, turning out sardonic articles, mostly about local politics, which the *Bay Shore Sentinel* bought for five dollars apiece and published under the pen name, Jolly Beane. Readers sent in irate letters, demanding to know where they could locate "this Jolly Beane." I was one of the few who knew, for I was the courier between Simmy's bay-boat office and Vic Scanlon, the editor of the *Sentinel,* for whom I eventually went to work. I kept my secret. Not even Sara knew.

Before Simmy would dispatch me to the *Sentinel* office, he would make me read his article first. "Here, check this over for grammar and punctuation, will ya, my good lad!" Like many yarn-spinners, Simm had no respect for obstructionist commas and periods. He plowed right past them, running his sentences and paragraphs together. But he was a shrewd observer. His articles would begin in a deceptive, light-hearted way, as if they were meandering nowhere, and then suddenly conclude with a trenchant comment on human nature.

Wes, who had no literary pretensions, lived in a rented room over a seafood restaurant across from Anson's. A red-faced man with tousled hair, he strode vigorously, as if he were bucking the wind even in a dead calm. When things were slow at Anson's, he could be found in the restaurant shucking oysters, sipping from a drink and roaring out orders as though he were commanding a cutter on a stormy day.

Despite their bad luck, Simm and Wes were high-spirited men, and nobody ever spoke ill of them or held them in contempt for their past. They weren't disgraced; quite the contrary, they were heroes, men who had delivered the goods in the face of a law that contravened nature and the proclivities of men, for there wasn't a bayman who didn't attribute his ruddiness to the holy trinity: sun, saltwater and rum.

With the exceptions of Oscar Boehme, that is. A squat, bowlegged man, Oscar was ship's carpenter at Anson's and spent his working days protected from the elements in a dilapidated shed that was once barn red but had long since weathered gray. Oscar had a reputation for steaming timbers in a long box and bending them onto sturdy oak ribs, all crafted with his own hands. If you wanted to affirm the character of your boat, it was enough to say she had been built by Oscar Boehme. Yet Oscar was oblivious to fame or the opinion of his peers. He worked for wages and warded off sin by whistling hymns all day long. He stopped whistling whenever he ran his band saw, but when the saw stopped humming the hymner started up again. A tactiturn man, he wasn't easily provoked except by the scent of whiskey. Once he detected a drop on the breath of a miscreant, he would deliver a sermon—and not on the way in which a combustible vapor might ignite the tinderbox in which he worked. To avoid his wrath, Simm and Wes gave the ship's carpenter a wide berth.

But Oscar didn't seem to mind if a boy wandered into

his shed and watched him work. He rarely acknowledged my presence, but he never kicked me out. Once, however, I remember him glancing my way and asking,

"What's your favorite hymn, son?"

I blurted out the first hymn that popped into my head.

" 'Rock of Ages,' sir."

He seemed well pleased. For the next hour he whistled "Rock of Ages" and, although I was stiff from sitting on a sawhorse, I didn't dare budge.

The boat he was building intrigued me. It had lines similar to the blue sloop I had seen so often under sail, except that she was half again as large. She had the same bright deck, the same shaped cuddy (enlarged to a trunk cabin) and the same underslung bow and stern. Simmy told me she was being built for a naval architect—for his own personal use—but that was all he knew.

Then one day I saw a trim man with a crew haircut enter Oscar's shed with what looked like a set of blueprints rolled up under his arm. I recognized him instantly as the skipper of the blue sloop, the helmsman who had ducked so neatly under the boom as the boat swung in a broad reach in front of the Coast Guard dock and then jibed toward home. I wanted to ask Oscar about the man and the boat he was building for him, but I didn't dare break through the concentration of his hymns and band saw.

Oscar tolerated Simm and Wes, but he despised Roy Anson, Jr., the red-eyed scion of the upright man who owned and ran the yard, which had been passed down through generations of Anson men. The yard, obviously, would not pass into the hands of Roy, Jr., for he was rarely sober enough to manage himself. At age 40, the only task Roy had mastered was throwing the switch that governed the winch that hauled the boats, once braced, up the ways. He would stand by the switch, his face covered with stubble, his potbelly protruding over his belt, his eyes bleary, and watch his father in the distance near the launching ramp. When old man Anson raised one hand, it meant cut the switch; when he raised both hands, it meant restore the power. Roy, the younger, could manage that much.

As it happened, the winch switch was located beside the band saw and Roy would station himself there, sneaking a nip from a pint bottle and blowing hot fumes in the direction of the ship's carpenter. Oscar, having long since abandoned all hope of saving the switch-thrower, would retreat to a remote corner of his shed with his brace and bits and start whistling "Onward Christian Soldiers" with a vengeance.

There was one other hand in the yard—a relic named Howie who was older even than old man Anson. A stooped figure with a nasal twang, Howie shuffled about the yard, stumbling over strewn timbers and slantwise bulkhead bracings, his wrists and ankles taped, his back bent, talking interminably to himself or anyone else who would listen. It took him a week to do what Simmy and Wes did in an hour, but Anson who had all but disowned his son was too tenderhearted to let him go. Howie had worked at the yard his entire life, and he would continue to work there until his arthritic knees collapsed under his frail frame.

As for old man Anson, he seemed at first to be a crotchety person with the prickliness that so often accompanies age—or so I believed. But as I got to know him better I realized his scowl was mostly a veneer that masked the disappointments of his days. The yard was going downhill; the sheds needed painting and the winch gears were threadbare and often slipped. But what was the use of sinking capital into a family business when there was no apparent heir? And so he went on doing his job as he had always done it, although he had long since forgotten why.

A solid, white-haired man of seventy, Anson was a past master at moving boats up and down the ways and sideways across his yard. He could move them on rails or he could slide them on greased boards; and he would do it all without ever touching a timber chock himself. He would stand with his arms straight at his sides, his fingers twitching behind his back, and bark, "Put a shim in her stern, Wes. Hold off now, until we get something underneath her bow. Simm, wiggle your tail before she takes a nose dive!"

"Nobody can haul a boat like Roy Anson," Simm confided in me one day. "That's what he majored in at engineering school."

I spent more time at Anson's that summer than sailing the bay. Part of it was justified, for *Lively Lady* required constant adjustment and repair. In addition to her other sins, she shipped water unmercifully through her centerboard trunk and there were times when it seemed as if I had the whole Great South Bay sloshing around inside. Ironically, even the weight of the water failed to sink the hippo to her waterline.

After a while I began to sail to Anson's out of force of habit; it was a destination, a place to pass the time in pleasant company. In late spring, Simm and Wes were

147

often too busy to talk, but by mid-summer the yard was practically deserted, except for the occasional boat that had to be hauled out because she had collected too many barnacles on her unpainted bottom or sprung a leak. Then the brothers would laze out of the sun under the wet hull, water seeping through the seams, and gab. Whenever I sailed up to the boatyard dock and dropped my sails, I would hear the echo of the caulking hammer and then, above it, the foghorn that belonged to Wes: "Halloo Rick!"—a hoarse siren call.

But there was something else that drew me to Anson's, and it had nothing to do with the boats or the men who caulked and painted them. Margery Hubbard lived across the narrow neck of waterway, so close I could scale a clamshell and hit the bulkheading behind her house. I knew I could count on seeing her every afternoon about three when Captain Schuyler Hubbard steered *Nimrod* down the creek with his party aboard. He always brought *Nimrod* to her berth in the same exact way. First he would scrape the mooring post along the port rub rail; then he would reach out with his left hand and grab the bow line draped over a post, securing it amidships, and then he would throw the engine into reverse and let the boat turn on its axis 180 degrees, using the post as a fulcrum. Bow and stern lines secured, he would step ashore, place a thick shellacked gangplank between the dock and *Nimrod*'s stern and graciously help the ladies ashore. After the last guest had departed, Margery would appear and help her father hose down the boat.

About that same time I would be aboard *Lively Lady*, which I always moored so that only about 30 yards of

148

creek separated her stern from the Hubbard dock. Seeing me there, Margery would wave, and when she finished swabbing *Nimrod*'s decks she would settle on the edge of the dock and we would chat. Her voice, her laughter, her lithe movements, her filial devotion—they all aroused in me a passion that I disguised. We were friends, good friends, but only friends. The narrow neck of water was like a moat to a castle I dared not cross.

"What brings you here today, Rick?" the Captain would ask, as if he didn't know.

"The shrouds parted at the deck," I would answer, or some such thing, which might or mightn't be so.

"She the darndest sloop I ever seen," he would say and stroll off, a hitch in his gait.

Margery would laugh at her father's comment, the brightness rising to her eyes. She was so serene, so artless, so easy to worship from afar. Her face was unclouded and if there was a shadow in her life, I didn't see it there. Yet I was beset by a demon, for even as we chatted so blandly I wanted to reach out and seize her mask and strip her bare. After a while she would say she had to go inside to help her mother, and I would hoist my sails and head for home, filled with desire and grateful I had such a sloop to divert my mind.

Uncle Bert grew restless as the summer days wore on. For a while he talked about buying a boat, but it was a foolish notion and he knew it, for he had nobody to run a boat for him and no inclination to learn himself. He was a born guest when it came to boating, even when it came to life, for he loved to be waited on. He didn't want to worry about mooring and anchoring and repairing a stalled engine in the middle of the bay with a storm coming on. But he was willing to pay somebody else to stew about what might go wrong.

Then one day it occurred to him that he could charter a boat, and when I told him about Margery Hubbard's father he picked up the phone and arranged for a sail aboard *Nimrod* the very next Saturday. He and Aunt Flo went out with the gracious Captain, and they enjoyed themselves so much they chartered *Nimrod* for the following Saturday too. Uncle Bert's mind was at ease once more, for he knew that no matter how hard he worked all week he could still gather up his weekend quota of sun and sea air. For the rest of the summer, and for many summers to come, he and Aunt Flo cruised the bay aboard *Nimrod* on Saturdays from nine to three.

Of course, I was delighted by this development because it strengthened the tenuous tie between Margery and myself. I began to feel I might yet cross that moat. Gradually a thought formed in my mind; I would ask Margery for a date—we could go to the movies. It was an obvious expedient; other boys asked other girls for dates all the time, but for some inexplicable reason I had assumed the same option wasn't open to me. For a long time I allowed the notion to fester, then one evening I took a deep breath and picked up the phone. She said yes, she would be pleased to go to the movies with me.

I walked from my house to hers, then together we walked from her house to the movies and, afterward, back to her house in the dark—and finally I walked alone all the way back home. I can't recall the film we saw, but I suspect it was a thinly veiled propaganda movie, for I

150

distinctly remember talking about the war on the way back to her house, the last thing on my mind. Margery expressed the opinion that the war would go on for a long time, and I disputed her, saying that she failed to take into account one thing: "The spirit of the American fighting man." Margery was too polite to refute this silly contention, but I kept insisting on my point because I didn't know what else to say. Actually I was wondering what would happen when I got her to her front door. Would she stop long enough to let me press my lips to hers or would she bolt inside? When the moment arrived, she turned quickly toward me, thanked me and disappeared. I was hurt. I was relieved.

I strolled toward the bay and stood on the town dock, listening to the gentle waves. A couple walked by, lovers; he had his arm around her shoulders and she had her arm around his waist. They paused under a street lamp, not caring, and embraced. She stood on her toes and wrapped her arms around his neck. I turned away and watched for the beacon from the Fire Island Light.

Was it me, or was it all that foolish talk about the war? I didn't know the answer, but I resolved to try again. The next time I asked her to the movies she said no, then no again, then yes, then no twice more. Sometimes she said she had "a prior engagement" and other times she said she was "terribly tired" and wanted a little time for herself. Each refusal crushed me, and I resolved that it was too painful to test myself that way. But I couldn't let the matter rest. I kept calling her and pushing myself, never once realizing that in my total absorption with the Captain's daughter I had cut myself off from every other girl.

151

And there were other girls—shy girls who glanced at me furtively across the classroom, brash girls who brushed against me with their swirling skirts. They were there for me as they were there for any other boy—except that, unlike other boys, I saw them and turned away. They weren't Margery Hubbard. As long as I exalted Margery Hubbard I could dismiss them from my mind, and the more I exalted Margery Hubbard the more distant she became.

One August afternoon I sailed to Anson's and found Simmy sitting on a sturdy chest on the bow of his boat, whipping a frayed rope end. We chatted for a bit, but I barely listened, for I was watching for a sign of *Nimrod* slipping down the creek on the far side of the yard. The creek was situated so that, from Simmy's mooring, I could only see the tops of boats that passed until they cleared the yard and emerged in full view. My eyes kept switching from Simmy's deft fingers to the passing boats. *Nimrod* was late—a treat for Aunt Flo and Uncle Bert but a nuisance for me. I was impatient, for I knew that if they didn't return soon I would have to sail off without seeing Margery. Indeed, I had returned to *Lively Lady* and was just about to raise my sails when the white peak of a mainsail, carrying the number 3, loomed above the bulkheading across the yard. The blue sloop swept into full view; the lean skipper brought her into the wind against a post and then tossed a line to old man Anson, who pulled the stern ashore.

"We'll just leave her here for a bit, Jed," Anson said, "and then we'll put her in the shed."

"Fine, Roy, that's just fine."

I walked up to the boat and watched the skipper as he

filled a bucket with fresh water from a nearby tap and then splashed it across his varnished decks.

"Hello," I said.

He paused and looked up. "Hello there."

"She's beautiful," I said.

"I'm glad you think so. Thanks."

He seemed a friendly, easy man in his early thirties.

"I've seen her many times."

"Have you."

"Yes, I have. Under sail out by the lighthouse and lots of other places too."

"You get around," he said and smiled.

"But I've never seen her here."

"Oh," he said, "I keep her behind my house in Great River. But now she's up for sale."

I felt my mouth turn dry.

"I can't imagine why," I said.

He looked at me, puzzled.

"I mean I can't imagine why you'd want to sell her."

"Oh," he said. "I've got a bigger one being built in that shed over there. I'm going to take her down the inland waterway."

I realized there were worlds beyond the world I knew, and they didn't interest me. The only world I cared about was bounded by the barrier beach at Fire Island and the mainland on the south shore. My world didn't extend farther west than Babylon or farther east than Bellport. That was world enough for me.

"I see," I said as he turned away and busied himself again. "How much?" I mumbled.

"Pardon?" he looked up, still smiling pleasantly.

"Nothing. I was just admiring her lines."

"She's been rebuilt," he said. "I did it myself. Put this deck on her a strip at a time." The deck was a work of craftsmanship, long mahogany strips, each about an inch wide and flowing with her graceful sheer.

I sat down on the bulkhead and watched him as he moved deliberately about the sloop. After he finished washing her down, he snapped the main halyard to the end of the boom and then raised it several feet, slipping a cradle underneath. He raised the centerboard, a small board that obviously slipped through a thick lead keel, and then he coiled all the halyards and hung them on a hook under the cuddy. Then he coiled the main and jib sheets on the deck. Finally, standing in the cockpit, he stuffed the sails loosely into a canvas bag, which he threw over his shoulder and stepped ashore. He remained on the edge of the dock for a moment, a final inspection, and then he said, "Yes, she sure is pretty and she's been good to me."

"I guess," I said, "you'd like to sell her to someone who would appreciate her as much as you."

"How did you know that?" he asked, and smiled in his easy, pleasant way again.

"Well," I said, "if she were my boat, that's how I'd feel. Of course, if she were mine I don't think I could bear to give her up."

"All things come to an end," he said. "Then you go on to something else. For me the 'something else' is in that shed, ready to be launched."

I supposed he was right, but I didn't feel that for me life had yet begun. I was ready for that blue sloop, I knew I was. But how much? How much?

I returned to Simmy who was still sitting in the self-

154

same spot, now splicing a loop in another rope.

"Simmy," I said, "you know all those articles I've run down to the *Sentinel* for you every week?"

He didn't raise his eyes from his splice. "I sure do kiddo," he said. "And now you want a favor in return, right?"

"Right."

"What is it?"

"I'd like you to find out for me what that sloop over there costs. It's up for sale."

Simmy kept on splicing. "Why get yourself all worked up about that, Rick?" he said. "You know your old man can't afford her. She's the prettiest Timber Point on the bay."

"I'd still like to know," I said. "Just for the sake of it."

"Just for the sake of knowing?"

"Just for the sake of knowing."

"And you promise, if I find out, not to get yourself all worked up about it?"

"I promise."

He put down his rope and walked over to the office where the elder Anson was usually holed up with paperwork. A few minutes later he was back.

"Fifteen hundred," he said and picked up his splice.

He might just as well have said a million. And yet it had to be. Somehow I knew it had to be, and I would have to succeed this time by myself, for I had lost Sara as an ally.

But it was fifteen hundred dollars, a sum so large that it struck me as a virtual impossibility. I couldn't approach Uncle Bert and ask him to lay out that much money for me.

155

I walked back to to where the blue sloop was moored and watched her tugging gently at her lines, nudged by the wake of passing boats. I studied her fittings—the way her main sheet wound through two sheaves on her boom and three, arranged in a triangle, on the aft deck. The jib sheet passed around winches and could be trimmed far aft. She was big enough to accommodate four with ease, but she was rigged so she could be sailed by one—alone.

But who was that one?

I glanced across the creek. To my amazement, *Nimrod* was already berthed and washed down and everyone had disappeared. To the west, the sun had already dropped behind the boat shed and now I would have to sail my hippo home in a dying breeze.

All that fall and winter I wandered down to the boat-yard whenever I could to see if the blue sloop had been sold. "Somebody was down here inspecting her yesterday," Simmy might say, "but I don't know who. I haven't heard." Whenever I learned that someone was looking at her I was filled with jealousy. I didn't want anyone touching her because she was mine, mine! But after the first snowfall Simmy set my mind at ease. "I don't think anyone will be buying her until spring," he said. "People don't think much about buying boats while all this white stuff is on the ground."

So I had until spring—a winter's respite from worry, but I had no plan. I was hoping, trusting that something would happen, that through some fluke she would fall into my hands. At the same time I felt powerless to

156

influence events, as if my fate lay in the hands of some arbitrary authority. "There's nothing I can do," I said to myself, "nothing at all." And knowing there was nothing I could do, I did nothing except entertain vague hopes and bide my time. I didn't mention the presence of the blue sloop to Sara or to Uncle Bert or Aunt Flo. Nobody knew about my secret yearning. Why tell them? What good would it do?

But I dreamed of the blue sloop and checked on her as often as possible. She was well protected in a shed where she sat high and dry between two cabin cruisers twice her size and many times her cost, but neither as alluring as she. I would run my hand down her smooth gunwales and along her leaded keel. Under sail, she had appeared as one kind of boat, and on dry dock as quite another. When she was in the water I admired the sweep of her deck up to her forceful prow, but in the storage shed I saw her from a different perspective and admired the slope of her tumble-home.

With the approach of spring my desperation became unbearable. The snows melted and the boatyard turned to mud, but that didn't deter buyers from milling about. Fortunately, most of them seemed less interested in boats powered by the wind than noxious gasoline. One day a boy about my own age, who had come to Anson's with his parents, stood staring at the blue sloop. "Look at this one, Pop!" he said and my heart leaped. The father glanced back over his shoulder and said, "The trouble with sailboats is that they take you too darn long to get there." The boy accepted his father's word as gospel. "Yeah, I guess you're right." If I hadn't been so relieved,

157

I'd have felt sorry for that boy, for I had already learned that the destination was the journey and not the stopping-place.

Then one day Uncle Bert came home from work and put a railroad ticket in my hand. It was toward the end of Easter holidays, and he told me he wanted me to take the noon train into the city, walk up to his office and that he would then take me to buy some summer clothes. "Everything you own is up to your elbows," he said, and it was true. I was fifteen; I would be sixteen in June. In the past year I had grown three inches and gained thirty pounds.

I rode on one of those off-hour trains that poked from station to station along the south shore while the conductor sang out the litany of their names in a nasal twang. "Amityville, Massapequa Park, Massapequa, Seaford, Wantagh . . ." and so forth. The pleasant hamlets with their quaint stations soon gave way to the grim tenements of Queens and then the long passage underground that I thought would never end. When I arrived at Penn Station my palms were black with soot from the open window and my face smudged.

I looked at a small map Uncle Bert had drawn for me and followed a checkered path underground to Sixth Avenue. I walked up a flight of subway steps and then headed uptown past Bryant Park until I reached Forty-Fourth Street, where I turned east toward Fifth Avenue. The further east I went the more stylish the buildings became, and when I finally reached the building in which he worked I was impressed by the heavy brass revolving door, the marble lobby and his name on the directory on the wall.

158

There were several other offices on his floor and I entered the one that had his name inscribed in black on the glass door:

BERTRAM MANN & COMPANY
TITLE SEARCH AND MORTGAGE GUARANTY

The words had power and substance even though I didn't know what they meant.

I had expected to find Uncle Bert sitting in a barren office waiting for the phone to ring. What I discovered when I entered startled me. One woman was sitting at a typewriter, rapping out a letter. Two other women were scurrying around the office, waving large legal documents and banging file drawers. Two phones were ringing at the same time and there was momentary confusion over who was going to take the calls, who was going to file the documents, who was going to type the urgent letter and who was going to attend to me. Finally, one of the women escorted me to Uncle Bert's inner office where he was sitting in his shirtsleeves behind a heap of legal papers, talking rapid-fire into the telephone and snapping his suspenders at the same time. His voice was crisp and direct, and when he finished with the first caller he hung up without saying good-bye and immediately started talking to the second caller without saying hello. As he spoke, he glanced down a document one of the secretaries had put in front of him, penciled a few notations in the margin and waved her off. This was an Uncle Bert I had never seen before.

He pointed at an upholstered chair on the opposite

side of his desk and I slumped into it. I glanced around his office and I began to think how each man has his habitat, his natural place where he feels most at home. For my father, it was behind an easel in a studio; for Uncle Bert it was behind a cluttered desk talking on the phone. And for me—for me it was on the windward deck out somewhere on the bay.

"Now Rick," Uncle Bert said at last, "you're going to be sixteen soon and it's time we had a business talk."

I had no idea what he was about to say, but I was pleased by the way he addressed me, as if I were an associate. But he ruined it at once by adding, "My gosh, you're coal black. There's a men's room out in the corridor. First door on your right. Go and wash up first!"

When I returned, he stepped around behind me and closed the door. Then he settled in a chair like mine, not behind his desk, and it was clear to me that he had made a mental adjustment. He wasn't Bertram Mann & Company, Title Search and Mortgage Guaranty. He was the Uncle Bert who had picked me up at camp and taken me to his home.

When our privacy was assured, he began tentatively, "There are some things you should know about—so you'll understand. You're aware, of course, that your Aunt Flo and I were appointed your legal guardians by court order shortly after your parents died."

"I know that, Uncle Bert."

"What you probably don't realize," he went on, "is that the court order authorizes me to use whatever monies you have to defray the cost of your upbringing."

160

He watched me closely and saw my surprise. And I was surprised, not so much by the information as by what it implied. It suggested that somewhere there was money for bringing me up.

"I didn't know that," I said.

"You see," he said, making a stab at humor, "it could be costly raising a boy with a voracious appetite like yours. So the court recognizes that the guardian oughtn't to be burdened with this expense if the child's parents have provided for him."

"I see," I said, not knowing what he was leading up to.

"Now," he went on, "as we know, your father was a fine commercial artist. One of the best."

"Yes, I know."

"But, Rick, it pains me to tell you this. He was a terrible businessman. Your father and your mother, they were fine people, full of fun. But they lived for the moment, only for the moment. I don't know how many times I said to your father: 'Les, you should take out life insurance—for the boy's sake.' And your father would always laugh and put me off. 'Bert,' he would say, 'what for? I'm a young man still. What for?' "

"I see," I said again, dropping my eyes. If there was no money, then why was he telling me this.

"Well, one day I induced your father to come to this office on some pretext or other. I forget what it was. He was sitting right where you're sitting now, and unbeknownst to him I had my insurance broker come here at the same time, and when I had the two of them together I went outside and locked that door and didn't open it again until my broker told me that it was all right, he had gotten your father to sign on the dotted line."

161

Uncle Bert was smiling. He had leaned back in the chair, his hands behind his head, and was staring up high at the molding on the wall.

"You see, Rick, your father was a terrible practical joker. Why when your Aunt Flo and I got married, do you know what he did? He managed to find out the name of the hotel where we were staying and he called us all night long. Every fifteen minutes he would call us on the phone. 'Everything all right, Bert,' he'd say. 'I'm just checking to make sure everything's all right.'"

Uncle Bert began to laugh until his eyes were moist. Then he blew his nose and got himself back on track again.

"Anyhow," he said, "I vowed someday I would get back at him. And I did. I locked him up with my insurance broker and I didn't let him out until he signed on the dotted line."

He chuckled and so did I. I didn't know what else to do.

"It wasn't that much of a policy," he said, "but it was better than no policy at all. Six thousand dollars, that's all it amounted to."

"Uncle Bert," I said, "I understand. You don't have to explain. If you have to use the money, that's all right. Don't worry, it's all right."

He jumped up. "My Lord, Rick, no! You misunderstand what I'm trying to say. Spend it? Never! I never spent a nickel of it! Not a nickel! It's all still there!"

"Still there?"

"I just want you to have an accounting—to know it's there. Oh sure, there were times when I thought I might have to dip into it. But I didn't, and now things are going

162

better, ever so much better, and it looks as if I won't have to touch it at all."

"Where is it—in stocks and bonds?" I asked knowingly.

"Stocks and bonds! Now you listen to me. I don't ever want to hear you talk about stocks and bonds. If you want to bet your money go to the racetrack, but I forbid you ever to put your money in stocks and bonds. Is that clear?"

"Yes sir."

"Now it's down at the Ninth Federal in an insured savings account where the interest accumulates regularly. That way it will be there when you need it someday."

He paused.

"You see," he said, "I have this idea. Someday you'll meet a girl and you'll marry her. When you do, you'll have the money intact to put down on a house. That will be a compensation. It will help make up for what you've lost. You'll have a wife and a house and a family of your own. That's why I want you to know the money is there."

I was too young and too excited to appreciate his sentiment. All I could think about was that I had six thousand dollars, plus accumulated interest. Six thousand dollars, and it was mine!

"Uncle Bert," I said, "I understand how you feel about the house and all that, but there's something I want even more than a house."

"What's that?"

"A different sailboat."

"Another boat! What's wrong with the one you have?"

"Uncle Bert, she's a terrible boat. A tub. She has a lee helm and she ships water . . ."

"Wait a minute! Don't spout all those nautical terms! I don't know what they mean."

"There's a lovely Timber Point for sale at the boatyard. I've seen her many times. I met her owner—he's a naval architect and he rebuilt her himself. She's a beauty, Uncle Bert. Jed—that's the architect—he's building a bigger boat and he wants to sell the Timber Point."

Uncle Bert was rubbing his chin and looking at me. "What's he asking?"

"Fifteen hundred."

He whistled between his teeth. "Fifteen hundred, that's a lot of money!"

"She's worth it, though."

"I'm not saying she isn't. But that's still a lot of money."

"But maybe we could take fifteen hundred out of the six thousand. Could we do that?"

I was afraid he was going to explode again, as he had over stocks and bonds. But this time he was quiet and firm, so firm that I dared not raise the matter again. "No," he said, "that's something we won't do. That money is set aside for you—for later on. I'm set on that point. I can't be swerved."

"But it's . . ." I began and caught my tongue.

He raised his eyebrows as if he guessed what I was about to say. I was about to say that it was my money, not his, and I'm glad I never finished what was on my mind. "I suppose you're right, Uncle Bert," I said instead, and he could see how downcast I was.

"How long have you known this boat was up for sale?" he asked.

"Since late last summer."

"And you never mentioned it?"

"No."

"But why? Why didn't you say something?"

"I don't know. My chances of ever getting it seemed so slim, and I didn't want to trouble you."

"But you could've asked," he said. "You could've asked." He took a deep breath, and seeing he would get no logical response from me, said, "Could we sell your present boat?"

"I don't see why not. Since we were dumb enough to pay three hundred for her, I suspect there are plenty of others just as dumb as we."

"If we got three hundred for it," he said, "then we would need to raise only another nine hundred and fifty."

"But that only makes twelve hundred and fifty, Uncle Bert," I said.

"Nine hundred and fifty, nine hundred and fifty," he kept repeating the number as if there were something magical about it, drumming his fidgety fingers on his dark oak desk. "Nine hundred and fifty. That might be possible. I might be able to swing that." Then he looked at me and came back to the task at hand.

"Now let's go out and get you some clothes," he said. "I want to get you a sport jacket and some slacks and a few shirts and a nice tie."

"I need some socks too, Uncle Bert."

"Socks?" he said. "I think I'll let your Aunt Flo take care of that."

165

It was a blustery April day when Uncle Bert met with Jed Harmon at Anson's shipyard. The wind in its perversity had shifted to the north, as if it were about to blow the departed winter back into our lives. The three of us ducked into the shed and stood beside the blue sloop.

"I'll tell you what," Uncle Bert said to Jed. "We like the boat. We want to buy it. We'll offer you twelve fifty firm."

Jed blanched at the directness of the attack. He was good-natured and Uncle Bert's sudden thrust threw him off guard.

"I'm really asking fifteen hundred," he said. "But I suppose I might give a little. Maybe a hundred or so."

"Twelve fifty. That's our offer," Uncle Bert said.

"Well, I don't know . . ."

"Twelve fifty. Cash on the barrelhead."

"I might go to thirteen," Jed said, "provided I can keep the spinnaker. I know somebody who will give me a hundred for the spinnaker alone."

"Twelve fifty," Uncle Bert said, "including the spinnaker. Including everything."

My heart was pounding at a terrific pace. I had no idea Uncle Bert could be so ruthless. He hadn't the foggiest notion what a spinnaker was. If it had been me, I would have let the spinnaker go and paid thirteen. I probably would've paid fifteen.

"I don't know," Jed said. He began to walk around in a small circle, as though he was confused. "You say you'll pay me now."

"I have a cashier's check made out for twelve hundred and fifty dollars. Either I give it to you or I rip it up."

Jed started to laugh. "I guess you'll have to give it to me. I couldn't bear to watch you rip it up." He turned toward me. "You'll like this boat," he said. "She's everything a boat should be, and now I'm glad she's yours. But you must promise me you'll take care of her decks and not let her go to rot."

"I'll take good care of her, Jed."

Then Jed shook my hand and Uncle Bert's hand and took the cashier's check and walked away. I sat down on a huge supporting timber under her keel and said, "She's mine, she's mine!"

"There's something you must promise me too," Uncle Bert said.

I looked up at him.

"When you want something you must go after it and bargain for it knowing you might lose it. Do you understand?"

"I understand," I murmured.

Then Uncle Bert looked at the blue sloop, as though

for the first time. "Good Lord," he said, "she's some hunk of machinery. First time out you'd better take somebody along who knows how to sail a boat this size!"

Jed had called the sloop *Miss Prim*—a prissy name. I named her *Circe*, after the enchantress, and now I yearned to fly with her down the wind.

One May morning Simm and Wes slid the sloop on greased skids out of the shed and into the yard. She appeared as alluring to me on dry dock as under sail. I circled her, admiring her hull from every perspective, keeping a respectful distance.

"You sure won't get nowhere gaping like that," Simmy said to me. He yanked the sandpaper from my hand, wrapped it around a small, flat block, and rubbed the mahogany coaming vigorously where the varnish had begun to peel. Then he handed the sandpaper to me. "Don't be afraid to touch her," he said. "She won't fall apart."

I began tentatively.

"Good night," Wes barked from the other side of the yard, "lean into it, boy!"

I began in earnest, going over every inch of her deck and hull. It took me two days to sand her down. When I finished my body ached and my face, neck and arms were like burnished bronze from the sun.

Simmy inspected my handiwork.

"You've got to go over that deck again," he said, "then give her a light coat of varnish, then sand her down a third time and give her another coat. Then at least once during the summer you're going to have to sand her down and varnish her again. After each sail, you've got to swab her down with fresh water, ya hear! If you let that deck burn black, you'll have to strip her down to bare wood, bleach her out and start all over again. What's more, she'll never be the same. So you take care!"

He walked away, then turned and gave me one parting shot: "Remember, the best time to varnish is on a high, dry day when the wind is from the north."

"Go on," Aunt Flo said when I told her about Simmy's admonition, "he's pulling your leg!" Whenever she drove me to the shipyard, she would say, "Let's hope you have a north wind for good varnishing today."

But Simmy was right, for one day, years later, I foolishly varnished the deck in a southeasterly that brought two days of mist and rain. The undried varnish trapped the moisture and the deck turned to milky blotches that cracked and scarred.

When I finished varnishing the deck, I painted the hull blue, the cuddy green and the waterline white. Then Simmy came along with a bucket and brush and applied copper red to her bottom to discourage barnacles from settling there. Her bottom was still damp red when Wes and Simmy pulled the chocks out from under the wheels. The trolley started to roll down the ways, slowly at first, then gathering speed, while I stood in the cockpit, my heart pounding, an oar in my hands. *Circe* bucked when she struck the water and her hefty timber braces floated free. Now, in her natural element, she was transformed. She glided stern-first into the creek, which was covered with oil slicks from the ferries and filled with debris. I felt the responsive weight of her bouyant hull under me. I shifted from amidships to the port side, half expecting her to lurch like *Lively Lady* and pitch me overboard. But *Circe* merely dipped slightly, a gentle curtsy, as if to acknowledge that I was there.

I paddled halfway around the shipyard to a narrow canal no more than 15 feet wide, where I tied *Circe* to the bulkhead. Beside the canal, a makeshift crane, its base buried in concrete, angled overhead, leaning so far over the water it seemed as though it might topple. Simmy secured the hook-end of the tackle to the strong, slender mast, which I had also sanded and varnished; then he hoisted the spar high and clear while Wes and I swung it upright and stepped it through the deck. Then we secured the stainless steel shrouds and the fore and aft stays. We twisted the turnbuckles just above the deck until the wires vibrated when Wes plucked them. He listened to their twang, like a musician in search of Middle C.

"Don't ever make 'em too tight," Wes said. "If you do, they'll pull the mast clear through the keel. Or they'll snap the peak in a stiff breeze. Always leave a little play."

I attached the boom myself, then hung it snugly in its cradle and coiled the sheets and halyards that had been threaded through the proper sheaves beforehand. My chores completed, I stepped ashore. Once again I was struck by the fact that *Circe* was one kind of boat in dry dock, another kind sitting at her berth, and yet another under sail. Like the weather and the wind, she had different traits and moods, and I didn't know if I could master them all.

Suddenly I realized she was sinking below her waterline. I leaped aboard and raised a floorboard. "She's shipping water! She's shipping water!"

Once again Wes' crackling voice carried across the yard. "Man the pumps, boy! Man the pumps!"

Jed had rigged up an ingenious hand pump that sucked water out of the bilge into the centerboard trunk (for *Circe* had a centerboard that slipped through her keel for extra stiffness when pointing high). But that small pump was mainly useful for bailing the minor amounts of water she took over the deck while under sail or after a rain. To cope with the water now gushing through her seams, I borrowed a huge galvanized pump with a great spout that lifted the inrushing water in a steady stream and put it back into the bay.

Circe shipped water for nearly a week, in lesser amounts each day. While I was in school, Simmy dutifully pumped her dry. Then, on Memorial Day, I walked into Anson's Boatyard with my sailbag slung over my shoulder and sponged her dry. She had swelled up tightly, and she was swaying at her berth, straining at her painter, bobbing on her waterline.

"First time out," Uncle Bert had cautioned, "you'd better take somebody along who knows how to sail a boat that size!"

First time out I sailed alone. The wind came up at ten knots that morning and surpassed fifteen by early afternoon. High to the west I could see the pennants fluttering over the Bay Shore Yacht Club, but there was a dead spot to the lee of Anson's under the sheds where I raised my sails. I drifted across the creek until I cleared the buildings that blocked the breeze. At last I reached that place where the wind swept down the unprotected creek and filled my sails. I was afraid the sudden burst would knock me down, but the blue sloop heeled easily and nosed up into the wind as if she possessed an intelligence of her own. Three quick tacks and I cleared the shipyard and entered the bay which was a mass of whitecaps from shore to shore. I sailed close-hauled, pointing toward the Fire Island Light, where I knew Captain Hubbard had anchored *Nimrod* with my aunt and uncle aboard.

I sat well up on the windward deck, as I had when I sailed my duckboat and *Lively Lady,* using my body as a counterweight. I had no idea that *Circe* was a sloop of a different kind. Each time she heeled, the weather helm brought the tiller so far to leeward that it slipped beyond my grasp. As the boat righted herself I would grab the tiller again, only to lose it when she heeled once more. I crossed the bay, yawing and luffing, afraid that if I moved off the windward deck the boat would capsize.

When I was about five miles off the mainland I saw the stubby *Nimrod.* I judged the tide was high enough so that I could cross the shoals without running aground. I sailed below *Nimrod*'s stern on a reach, then headed up into the wind on her port side, leaving ten feet between the two hulls. It seemed a safe distance but I was wrong. I threw a line to the waiting captain, then dropped the mainsail, my second error. The strong wind filled my jib and turned my bow into *Nimrod*'s gunwale, gouging out a hefty chunk of planking.

The captain let out a wail. "It was your jib that done that! Always lower your jib first and let your mainsail luff!" He seemed more vexed by my indiscretion than by the damage to his hull.

With that, the captain fetched a saw from *Nimrod*'s

172

toolbox and stepped aboard my sloop, seizing a shroud for balance. He was a portly man of sixty with a gimpy gait, but he moved across the heaving deck with catlike agility. When he reached the cockpit he promptly sawed my six-foot-long tiller in half without permission or ado. "Too long," he said by way of explanation, then indicating the roiling waters, added: "In this light breeze you want to sit down here on the leeward side."

He positioned himself in the corner of the cockpit and ordered me to raise the sails and cast off. He sat with the truncated tiller over his right shoulder, extending beyond his ear. He didn't seize the stick but held it lightly between his thumb and forefinger as if listening to the sound of the water rising through the rudder post into his fingers.

"You've got to climb the wind," he said. "When you sail a boat, you've got to climb the wind all the time."

He told me that by sitting on the lee side I could see the peak of the jib. "Sail with the jib," he said. "Watch the jib way up high. Let the boat climb the wind until the jib luffs ever so lightly, then ease off a hair. Then, as the boat gains momentum, climb the wind some more."

Years later I read technical explanations in sailing texts about "real" and "apparent" wind. The able skipper sails the breeze the boat creates as she surges ahead. But it was from Captain Hubbard's vivid imagery— "Climb the wind!"—that I first perceived that delicate balance between boat, sail and sea.

When we sailed back to *Nimrod* he said: "You want to always lay her up close enough to crack an egg"—and crack an egg he could have. He left barely inches between his boat and mine. This time I let the jib down at once. I threw a bow line to Uncle Bert, and we lay nose up to the wind, mainsail luffing pretty as you please. The captain had been aboard just ten minutes, yet he had already taught me the two most valuable lessons of my sailing life: how to "climb the wind" and how to "crack an egg."

I whisked home with the wind behind, the swells running up my stern. I returned not to the shipyard but to the long Brightwaters Canal. As I neared my mooring post, I realized I had barely enough room to swing below it and head back up into the wind. There were too many other boats docked alongside, blocking my way.

I decided to come about above the post, lower my sails, and drift bare-masted downwind. It was a tactic I had performed successfully many times before with *Lively Lady*. But *Lively Lady* didn't generate the momentum that came from a leaded keel. As *Circe* coasted downwind she gathered awesome speed. Either I would have to crash into my mooring post or coast past it and figure out how to get back upwind again. Wisely, I chose the latter course, but once I was below my post I couldn't raise my sails because the wind was blowing over my stern, pushing me farther away from where I wanted to be.

A group of amused boatmen, seeing my plight, gathered along the bulkhead and shouted conflicting instructions:

"Paddle ashore!"

"Lasso a post!"

"Abandon ship!"

I was about to throw an anchor overboard when a small boy in an outboard launch came along and towed me back to my mooring. I sat in my cockpit, facing away from the shore, thoroughly disgraced.

A southeasterly gale blew for three days, driving the rain and the delicate shore birds before it. When the storm passed, a light breeze sprang up from the barrier beach, carrying with it the pungent aroma of tidal bog. The fever was on me, and I went down to my sloop and raised her sails.

In summer the prevailing breeze on the Great South Bay is from the southwest, and it rises and falls with diurnal regularity. It picks up at mid-morning, wafting the shore gently as the sun heats the land, and it gathers force through the long afternoon. In the evening after the sun sets, the wind drops off again, as if it were saving itself for a stiffer blow the next day.

I felt my best tactic was to catch the freshening breeze on the rise and sail close-hauled to Fire Island while the sea was flat. I pointed for the water tower at Saltaire, a silvery globe suspended in air. When I reached the lee shore the wind was brisk as I had hoped, but the sea was calm. I could see the bay-chop across the shoals to the north and sputtering whitecaps all the way to the mainland. But here under the barrier beach, where the white dunes rose, I had deep water and a stiff breeze and no waves: ideal sailing conditions for the novice I now admitted I was.

I had a two-mile stretch of open water between the lighthouse to the west and a string of islands to the east. All that morning I practiced tacking and jibing until I felt I was part of the boat and she was part of me. I sat on the lee side of the cockpit, the way the captain taught me, and watched the leech of the jib way up high. Like the captain, I sensed the rush of water past the rudder and the tiller came alive in my hand.

"Don't have a heavy hand," the captain had said, "don't oversteer!"

I discovered when I could let *Circe* sail herself and when she needed a gentle nudge from me. While tacking, I discovered I could leave the main sheet cleated when tending the jib. As long as she had enough headway, she would point up until both sails luffed, then slip across the face of the wind until they filled again on the other side. I could run, reach or tack, adjusting the sails for each maneuver with ease. The boat had been built for one man to sail alone—me!

Tiring at last, I sailed a broad reach eastward between a string of islands and the barrier beach along a narrow arm of the bay. On the southwest tip of the first island, known as West Island, a deserted beach house—a victim of the mighty hurricane of 1939—tilted forward, its porch submerged and the water lapping into its living room. I veered shoreward for a closer look—too close! My centerboard bounced on the sandy bottom and popped up through the trunk. In another moment my keel would strike and I would be stuck fast on a bar. I jerked the centerboard all the way up and trimmed the mainsail, and *Circe* swung upwind of her own volition toward deeper water. I realized then that my centerboard was as good a sounding device as a sonar beam. I didn't need electronic gadgets or gasoline engines to take me where I wanted to go. All I needed was a fair breeze.

I skimmed past Fair Harbor, Ocean Beach, Seaview—

176

beach communities nestled in the dunes. I moored in a large bulkheaded basin at Point O' Woods, incorporated as a private club and bordered by a barbed-wire fence to keep out the hoi polloi. But I knew there was unimpeded access to its pristine sands from the bay. It was as if the exclusive property owners there were saying: "If you come by land, keep out! But if you come by water, welcome to our sidewalks and our sea!"

I hiked the half-mile across the barrier beach, swam in the chill ocean, drowsed on the hot sand; then I sailed home roundabout the easterly end of the island string, south to the mainland and west to Bay Shore. I shot down my arrow-straight canal and came up to my mooring, not too fast and not too slow. Nobody witnessed my perfect landing. Where were all the amused spectators now?

In the days that followed I found out something fundamental about myself: I was a lazy sailor at heart. I had no yen to race, to command others, to cross the ocean single-handed; I merely wanted to cruise this precious jewel, the Great South Bay, with my sheets cleated while the sea swirled over the lee rail. I wanted to venture down hidden creeks and harbors, to explore islands, to watch for the wading heron or the erratic flight of the rattling kingfisher as he burst from a reedy shore. I lived only for the sultry southwind that induced a languor in my youthful bones. I had no desire for companionship. I sailed alone.

School ended; July and August stretched before me like all eternity. I had nothing to do, no place to go, except to sail. I had but one rule: never set the same course two days in a row. Each morning I caught the freshening breeze and tacked out of the narrow canal. By now I knew exactly how close I could come to the bulkhead on either side before coming about. But it wasn't until I cleared the last jetty that I made my impulsive decision: east, west, south or points in between—I didn't know my heading until I set my sails.

One blustery afternoon—the southwest wind had been kicking up for five consecutive days—I raced past the lighthouse toward Fire Island Inlet and the open sea. I remembered the difficulty Sara and I had in our frail duckboat, bucking the wind, current and tide. But *Circe* had the surge and power to maintain her leeway against the swells, rising over the crest of one wave and knifing through the next. As the barrier beach narrowed, I could hear the relentless pounding of the breakers; I envisioned the expanse of ocean beyond the surf, so endless, so enticing, so far removed from the demands of civilized society. But when I approached that point where bay and ocean met, I saw how the cross-currents swirled treacherously around the ever changing bars, and I turned and ran with the wind and tide astern for the protected waters of the bay.

For a while after that encounter I didn't cross the bay at all. Instead I combed the mainland, explored its coves and creeks and skimmed its beaches. I would observe the bathers, standing waist deep in the water as they stared at my passing sloop the way I once stared at other sloops, filled with envy and despair. It was perversity and false pride that made me sit high on the windward deck at such moments so that the swimmers could see who was sailing by.

One hot July morning I drifted like the Ancient Mariner,

As idle as a painted ship
Upon a painted ocean

off a sandy point where bayberries grew. To my surprise, I saw another Timber Point class sloop like my own, except she didn't have a cuddy, drifting a quartermile away. She was skippered by an elderly man under a broad-brimmed straw hat and he had two young children aboard, a boy about ten and a girl about eight. Like me, they lay motionless, waiting for the reluctant wind to rise.

I saw the breeze before I felt it, rippling the still surface as it swept across the bay. The other sloop, more to windward, caught the puffs first; she heeled as her sails filled and the two children clapped their hands and the old man doffed his straw hat to the unseen genie of the winds, as though he were giving thanks.

Sometimes I would let Sara join me in these adventures, but only infrequently. She knew *Circe* was my sloop, that I had acquired her with my own wits, and that I wasn't beholden to her for her acquisition. Usually she jumped at my invitations, but one day she declined. "No, I don't think so. I've grown tired of sailing. It's such a bore." I took her at her word and sailed alone.

And so aloneness became a virtue, a way of life. Whatever I experienced alone, I alone possessed. When *Circe* lay over on her lines, she did so for me alone. The sound of water rushing past her hull was intended for my sole delight. Her wild downwind rides exhilarated me, and only me. I believed I couldn't share these feelings without spoiling them. Sailing was a solitary sport. And yet, as I sailed, I often caught myself pointing to the contours of the land, the changing complexion of the water, the alterations in the clouds, as if I had an imaginary person aboard who understood what my worldess gestures meant.

When my loneliness became more than I could bear, I would head for Oak Island, hoping to find solace in that place apart where the wind rose and my sailing life began. I would sail past Gwen's summer house, and although I often saw signs of life I lacked the boldness to tie up at her dock and clamber ashore. Then, one August day, as I entered the narrow estuary that flowed past the Gowan dwelling, I saw my old demasted duckboat drifting in the middle of the channel. Frank Gowan was aboard, half asleep in the noonday sun, with a long bamboo rod in his hand. His slack line was attached to a blue and white float, and I knew he was waiting for the snapper schools that had started to run. Gwen was sitting disconsolately on the dock, watching her father's bobber, her chin in her palms and her elbows on her knees. Her legs dangled over the edge of the rickety pier, and her toes disturbed the surface calm of the water, now at flood tide. She, too, had a bamboo rod, but it was sitting beside her on the rough-hewn planks. If Gwen wasn't fishing, then there were no fish lurking in the deep.

"Catch anything?" I said to Mr. Gowan. *Circe* had slipped up so quietly he didn't know I was there until he heard the luffing of my sails.

"Why Rick!" he said with surprise as he twisted around, and then sizing up my sloop, added, "Why, you sure have come a long way in the world."

180

"Only in terms of boats. Is Gwen around?" I asked, as if I hadn't the slightest idea she was less than fifty yards away.

"Well," he drawled, "I guess if you have eyes in your head you can see her sitting on the dock over there."

As I sailed up, Gwen tilted her head and folded her arms across her chest. A supressed smile spread across her lips and moved into her eyes. I tossed a bow line and it landed in her lap. She took a couple of quick turns around a cleat, and then stood up, holding the free end in her hands.

"Well," I said, "are you coming aboard or not?"

"Dad," she called hoarsely across the creek, "I'm going for a sail with Rick. All right?"

Mr. Gowan, his back to us, raised one arm over his head and waved us off, then slumped further under his long-peaked fishing cap.

Gwen pushed the bow away from the dock with her foot as she stepped aboard, and we skimmed eastward past the houses along the shore. She sat on the edge of the cuddy, her bare legs folded in front of her, and fixed me in her gaze. I could still detect the faint amusement in her mouth and eyes. I felt as though she had been trying to conjure me up and she was now pleased with herself that she had made me materialize.

"Hello," she said at last.

"Hello yourself," I replied.

"Nice of you to stop by."

"Yes, I kind of think so, too."

"Where are you taking me?"

"The name of this sloop is *Circe*," I said. "All questions of destination must be put to her."

"Is that the way it works?"

"That's the way it works. We must go where *Circe* takes us, and we must never question *Circe*'s course, for she knows best."

I steered into the State Boat Channel. We cut through the wake of a passing cabin cruiser; the fine salt spray collected on Gwen's tanned skin and glistened in her sun-bleached hair. She lay on her back, draping her legs over the edge of the cuddy. She rolled over and stretched prone, bending her knees and swinging them freely in the air. After a while she swung around and faced me again, her elbows extended and her chin on the backs of her hands. I hadn't spoken to her since the day I had tried to wipe the mascara from her face. She was leaner and longer, more serene and mysterious, and more aloof.

"You're still mad at me," I said.

"A little," she agreed.

"I apologize," I said.

She didn't respond.

"After all, if you want to mess up your pretty face with all that glop, that's your business, not mine."

She was smiling, trying not to smile, the light of laughter rising in her eyes.

"The truth is," she said, "that I wore all that glop, as you put it, because I knew it would make you ripping mad."

"Then you accept my apology?"

"Not yet. I want to savor it. I want to make you squirm." She slipped into the cockpit and sat on the floorboards, facing me. Our legs stretched toward each other. As I inched my leg toward hers, she inched hers away. Yes, she was a conjurer; she had powers over me I didn't understand.

I sailed toward the tip of Captree Island until the fallen timbers of the Wa Wa Yonda Club appeared above the dunes. When the centerboard struck bottom, I yanked it up, headed into the wind and Gwen heaved the anchor overboard. I lowered the jib and let the mainsail luff, and we waded ashore.

"I always wanted to see what this old place looked like," I said.

"It was a well-known hunting club at one time," she said. "Daddy says that duck hunters from all over Long Island gathered here every fall."

"I always heard it was a casino during Prohibition days."

"I guess it was that too."

We made our way gingerly in our bare feet over a rotted boardwalk stretched across marsh grass. Farther inland the weathered building leaned and creaked as I pushed open a warped door with a faded NO TRESPASSING sign tacked to it. Inside the floors were covered with blown sand and the walls and ceilings sagged.

"I don't think it's safe in here," Gwen said.

"If it has been standing this long," I said, "it won't come tumbling down now." I had her inside and I wasn't going to let her get away.

The structure wasn't large, about five rooms in all, but the only furnishing still intact was an old oak bar that had stood the test of salt and time. The rest of the building was bare, ravaged by vandals and the winds. Toward the rear of the barroom, a large paneless window frame overlooked the marsh, the reeds and the dunes, which

183

seemed to roll and flow like waves. Gwen stood by the window, intrigued by the view, and I came up behind and touched her arm. She moved away, but I grabbed her hand and pulled her toward me. The room was hot and still as she turned around and I touched her hair. She let me kiss her once and then she backed away.

"That's enough," she said. I remembered that day in the deserted dory and I was determined not to let my chances evaporate a second time.

"That's enough," she repeated, but she still had the enticing laughter in her eyes.

"Just once more."

"That's all! That's all!"

I had her around the waist, but she escaped. I seized her arm again, but she struggled free. I wanted to grab her ankle, to trip her up, but she was too agile for me. She ran through the open door into the sunlight. I pursued her over the boardwalk, and then I felt the jagged pain and howled. A splinter had pierced the sole of my foot and I danced on one leg.

"Here, let me see," Gwen said. She jerked my foot so far behind my back she nearly tipped me on my head.

"Take it easy, will you!"

"Oh yes," she said, "it's nicely imbedded in there."

"Can you get it out?"

"Sit down and I'll see what I can do."

We both sat down on the boardwalk. I rested my leg across her lap. "Can you see it?"

"I can see it, but can I get it out? That's the thing."

She removed a hairpin and began to probe. I jerked my heel.

"Hold still, will you please!"

"That pin isn't sterilized. You're going to give me an infection. I'll get gangrene and lose my leg."

"Do you want me to take this splinter out or not?"

"Take it out!"

She held my toes firmly while she scraped my callused sole. "By the way," she said, "who's that girl I see you talking to all the time after the basketball games?"

"What girl?"

"A pretty girl with dark brown hair."

"Oh, that must be Mar—ouch, Gwen, darnit, you're hurting me!"

"Don't be such a crybaby. What's her name?"

"Margery Hubbard."

"Do you like her?"

"She's all right."

"But you do like her. I can tell."

"Gwen," I said, "who's that boy I see you talking to all the time."

"He's not my boyfriend."

"He's not?"

"No. My boyfriend is 19. He's a sophomore in college."

"Gwendolyn," I said, "you don't have a boyfriend who's a sophomore in college. Why do you say things like that?"

"I do so. He's studying to be a doctor. And don't call me Gwendolyn," she said, jabbing the pin into my foot.

"Gwen!" I said.

"Hold still," she replied.

"Gwen," I said, "I have a great idea. Why don't the four of us, Margery and I and you and your boyfriend, whoever he is, go out together some time?"

"I've got a better idea," she said, holding the extracted

splinter up to the sun and examining it.

"What's that?"

"Why don't you go down to the edge of the water and soak your foot."

As we headed back to Oak Island, her humor changed. A darkness came across her face and the light went out of her eyes. She was like seawater that transformed itself with each passing cloud. But unlike the shoals and channels I knew so well, I couldn't read her moods. She might be tranquil on the surface and turbulent inside. She was a fascinating sea creature, half woman and half girl.

She sat on the cuddy with her back to me, watching the passing boats and the barren shore. "Gwen," I asked, "what's the matter?" I touched her hair and she brushed my hand aside. As I glided up to her dock, she jumped ashore and walked toward her house without turning around.

I wondered what I had done wrong. If I didn't kiss her, she threw me off the dock, and if I did she stalked off without saying goodbye. "Why can't she be more like Margery Hubbard, so sweet, so chaste," I said to myself as I sailed home alone across the bay.

Once a week I would sail to Anson's Boatyard and tie up behind Simm Wicks clamboat, the *Ballyhoo*. Invariably I would hear the clacking of his typewriter in the darkened cabin where he was still turning out an endless stream of sardonic articles for the *Bay Shore Sentinel*.

"Haloo Simmy," I would call, my voice echoing down the creek.

"Haloo Rick," he would say, and shortly appear on

deck with a manuscript in hand. Then I would sit on his deck and go over his story, inserting commas, periods and other punctuation marks before delivering it to Vic Scanlon later that day. Meanwhile, Simmy would scrutinize my sloop to make sure she was shipshape.

"Lookee here, Rick," he said one day, "what are you doing with a figure-eight knot at the end of your main sheet?"

"That's to keep the strands from unraveling," I said.

"You've got to whip those rope ends," he said. "Don't you know how to whip rope ends? Better yet, make an end splice. Splicing is better than whipping, and whipping is better than knotting. Remember that!"

Then he sat on a wooden box on his foredeck and showed me how to tuck the strands back into the standing part of the line, twisting until he had a handsome braid. "Now," he said, "you've got to learn the stomp and roll."

"The stomp and roll?"

He dropped the splice in the dirt and stomped on it and rolled it under his heavy work shoe. "That makes it good and snug," he said.

Later that day I put an eye splice in my painter and end splices in all my sheets and halyards, and they never unraveled or slipped through the sheaves again.

One hot August afternoon, as I sailed past the dead spot behind Anson's yard, I silently lowered my jib and slipped alongside *Nimrod*, taking Margery Hubbard by surprise. She was facing away from me, helping her father swab his decks, and she jumped when she realized a sailboat had docked off *Nimrod*'s port side.

"C'mon," I coaxed, "hop aboard!"

187

"Oh no," she said, "I couldn't."

"G'wan," her father urged, "she's seaworthy, she won't sink."

Margery put a bandanna over her pretty head and stepped carefully aboard, steadied by my hand. I was amazed at my bravura—sneaking into the captain's slip and stealing his daughter away. Whenever I sailed down Anson's Creek to visit Simmy, I would also watch for Margery, and I resolved that if I saw her I would sail right into the captain's berth and whisk her away.

I had long wanted to lure her onto my sloop. As part of my fantasy, I saw her hair blowing in the wind as she laughed at the salt spray. I imagined that in one moment of supernal joy we would realize we were meant for each other and find ourselves in a wild embrace while *Circe* fluttered in the breeze.

But we were barely out of Anson's Creek when I had to face up to the impossibility of that dream. She didn't like it, she didn't like—the captain's daughter didn't like to sail! I could tell by the way she gripped the coaming and winced in the spray. Each time *Circe*'s bow dipped into the trough of a wave, she huddled deeper into the corner of the cockpit and her face turned pale.

"Are you all right?" I asked, masking my disappointment, trying to show concern.

"I'm fine," she insisted, "just fine."

"Why don't you sit up here on the deck where you can see out over the waves?"

"It's too wet," she said.

But after a while she took my advice; the saltwater trickled down the deck under her bottom, and there's nothing like a salty bottom to raise an itch. I offered her a boat cushion and she sat on that. She smiled wanly, as if she were obliged to enjoy herself for my sake, for Margery was that way, but I knew there would be no hugging on deck that afternoon. "Why can't she be more like Gwen Gowan," I said to myself, "so impulsive, so free."

I came about and returned to Anson's Creek, and she thanked me "for the lovely sail" as she reached out for her father's hand, but I could tell she was genuinely relieved. I knew then I had been right all along. It was better to sail alone.

9 ~

One early September morning I sailed eastward along the coast. From a half-mile offshore, the land appeared heavily forested, almost primeval, as if it had never been crossed with steel tracks and paved streets. It was populated with soaring oaks, maple, elm, aspen and beech; stringy black willows leaned with the prevailing summer wind along the banks of creeks. As far as I could see over the tops of the swaying trees, the foliage extended inland. Here and there a house or a church steeple loomed through the leaves; but other than these incidental signs of civilization, the lush shore seemed untouched by human habitation.

I sailed against the climbing sun under a sky so clear I thought I could reach out and touch each separate leaf, each twig on the verdant shore. It was one of those deceptive cloudless skies that conveys not a hint of the storm to come, one of those mornings in which one must muster all one's sentience just to bear witness to the moment at hand. I scooped up a bucket of water and doused my head, to feel the salt on my face, its taste on

190

my tongue. I had put my faith in the healing power of brine. It tinged my cuts, bleached my brow and drew the poisons of loneliness from my soul.

I slumped into the cockpit, the tiller over my right shoulder, and glanced toward shore under the arching boom. The wind was blowing over the aft starboard quarter. I boiled along on a broad reach, past Timber Point where my boat had been built a quarter-century earlier; past the gaping mouth of Great River where only a few weeks before hundreds of sailboats from all over the bay had congregated for Race Week. Now the bay was largely deserted except for a gaff-rigged schooner under my port bow, scattered clam boats at anchor across the shoals, and swift, low-slung ferries slicing across the bay, leaving behind steep wakes that rolled interminably toward the shore. One such ferry, bound for Sayville, passed fairly close, and a lone passenger leaning against the rail, a businessman wearing a white shirt and tie, his suit jacket slung over his arm, waved to me as he churned by.

I sailed eastward, never imagining the weather would turn. This was only the second day of a fresh southwesterly that was sure to blow and build for a week at least. That had always been the pattern before, and I saw no reason why it should vary now. The summer wind was the one constant in my unsettled world.

The sun came over the top of the mast and I put on a hat with a long peak, which I had painted white, to protect my blistered nose. I sailed past Heckscher State Park where droves of children, many of them bussed from Manhattan's slums, swam on a sandy beach that was always littered with scraps of yellow, lettucelike seaweed. Farther eastward I sailed past the fields of La-Salle Military Academy where uniformed cadets drilled under the sun. I could hear the marching band and I could see the impeccable lines of youths on parade and I was glad I wasn't one of them.

I ate a sandwich and from a thermos gulped some fresh fruit juice that Aunt Flo had mixed especially for me. Toward noon I was gliding past Bayport in clear defiance of advice I had received from Simmy Wicks. "Now Rick," he had said, "never cruise too far downwind because, you know, that's easy sailing but you've still got to come about and tack back home." All that morning I put Simmy's admonition from my mind. The warm wind over my shoulder lulled me into a forgetfulness that only an untroubled boy can know. *Circe* skimmed eastward. Now and then I would say to myself: "Well, I guess it's time to come about," but I was going with the wind and I couldn't bring myself to push the tiller toward the sail and head up, as easy as that maneuver was.

Finally I approached Patchogue where a huge oil tanker, riding high and fast, was coming out of the harbor, and I knew I had sailed as far to the east as I cared to. But instead of heading home, I pointed toward the barrier beach, the land of desolate islands and dunes so different from that other shore. I decided to skim the beach communities; then, late in the day, with the wind astern again, make my final run for the Brightwaters Canal.

It wasn't until I was directly off the barrier beach that I first saw the thunderheads far out to sea. The black sky was curled back on itself, like a tidal wave rolling inexo-

192

rably toward shore. Was that thunder or the crash of waves? I told myself it was the pounding surf, for there was no flash of lightning on the horizon, only the ominous stampede of nimbus clouds. And yet under my particular patch of sky the sun was still shining, the wind still blowing southwesterly as it had all day.

I was off the boat basin at Point O' Woods when the wind disappeared. I lay flat becalmed, my sails limp, my boom flopping aimlessly from side to side. I had never known the wind to succumb so early in the afternoon. I had no choice except to wait as the thunderheads rolled across the barrier beach—but there was no thunder, only the roar of undetected wind. I was poised, watching the water carefully, not knowing from which direction the gust would come. I suspected the northwest and tried to keep *Circe* pointed in that direction, but I guessed wrong. The squall came out of the southeast and it knocked us down. *Circe*'s mainsail struck the water and I was nearly pitched overboard. Somehow I managed to free the snarled sheets and she popped upright again because of the counterweight in her keel.

The next thing I knew we were racing for the ferry slip at Ocean Beach amid deep swells that overtook my sloop and washed across her stern. *Circe*'s weather helm was overpowering, and my arm ached from battling the tiller as I tried to hold my course. First I was afraid of capsizing, then I was afraid of sinking, and then I was afraid of running aground. And now I was afraid I would plunge headlong into the wharf.

I aimed for the narrow opening that led into the basin; then, all at once under my sail, I saw the huge two-tiered ferry bearing down on me. The ferry and I were destined to arrive at the opening at the same time and there wasn't room for us both. Since I was without power, I had the right away, but I had never known a ferry boat captain to let a mere sailboat get the best of him. Might was on his side; he could barge me out of his way and squash me against the pier. Way up in the safety of his pilot house, he blew his horn and I could see him furiously waving me off. But where did the darn fool want me to go! He hadn't left me enough space to head up in that awesome wind and I certainly wasn't going to jibe. Just as imperiously, I waved him off—an act born more of desperation than temerity. By now both tiers were lined with spectators, watching this David and Goliath contest over who was going to enter the basin first. At the last moment I heard the giant engines groan and the ferry's props began to churn the water the opposite way. The big boat backwatered as I shot across its bow into the protected waters on the lee side of the wharf.

I came up to a mooring post, seized it with my boat hook and slipped the spliced bight of my painter over the top. My sails were luffing so fiercely I thought they would shred. I managed to lower them without tearing them, remove them from their spars and stow them under the cuddy just ahead of the driving rain. Cold and shaken, I put on my slicker and jumped ashore, making *Circe*'s stern lines fast to the cleat on the dock. I knew I was destined to spend the night at Ocean Beach, but at least my sloop was secure and I was safe.

I didn't have any money, but the girl with black hair behind the counter in the coffee shop didn't seem to mind. She said she had watched me sail into the harbor in my sleek sloop and she loved the way I forced the ferry boat to respect my right of way. For that feat alone, she said, I deserved a cheeseburger with pickles and as much coffee as I could drink to chase the shivers from my spine. In return, she made me promise I would come back one day and take her for a sail.

"I sure will," I said.

"Now don't you forget," she replied.

She was wearing a flimsy bodice and a flowing dirndl skirt and sandals that clumped noisily when she moved, revealing the curve of her instep. I judged she was in her early twenties, and I convinced myself—in light of my deed of daring-do—that she assumed I was too. I wanted to look at her longingly. But I didn't let on. I thought she would be appalled if she knew what was going through my mind.

Afterwards I sat on a bench in front of the coffee shop and waited for the black-haired girl. She didn't know I was waiting, but I waited anyhow. Toward evening the rain let up, the wind abated and a sultriness filled the air. The main drag of the beach community ran in front of me, two blocks long. At one end there was a hardware store and at the other end a fancy restaurant, a clapboard building with a blue and white awning stretched over a terrace where patrons sat in shirt-sleeves eating steamers and drinking.

The boat slip was directly in front of me and I could see *Circe*'s mast bobbing up and down beyond a raised-deck cruiser that had berthed alongside. Across the way the ferries docked to discharge their passengers before returning to the mainland to gather still more. I watched the people who disembarked—all shapes, all kinds. And nearly everyone was in a festive mood, as if they had been gearing themselves all week for the final Labor Day fling before their summer came to a close.

Some of the arrivals went into the coffee shop where the black-haired waitress was now busier than ever. Others went into Sis Norris', the bar next door, from which place I began to hear the light tones of a piano and voices in song. These weren't the carousing voices of drunkards but the full-bodied voices of people who loved to sing and clearly knew how. Lured by the voices, I pressed my face against a steaming window pane and rubbed the glass, peering inside. The first thing I saw was a goatish man sitting at a table by the upright piano, keeping time to the music by waving a filled beer glass through the air. He seemed to be in mock song: his mouth moving, his bushy brows working, his arms and torso reflecting and exaggerating the nuances of the song without uttering a sound. I was amused by his performance and he sensed he had an appreciative audience. Suddenly he turned toward me and, with the light of recognition, waved me inside, as if he knew exactly who I was, as if we were old friends and he had been expecting me. When I pulled back, he bounded out of the chair, as if propelled by springs, and in one soaring leap reached the screen door and poked his head outside. The remarkable thing was that the glass was still in his hand and still filled with beer. He was wearing a maroon slipover and white pants, the former pulled snugly across his barrel chest and the latter across his muscular thighs, and he reminded me of the gymnastic men I had seen clambering off the ferry a short while before.

196

He made a globular motion with his hands, his bony fingers outstretched, as if he were casting a spell; then he made a fist, and with his thumb extended like a hitchhiker, indicated the interior of the bar. For a moment I thought he was mute, for I had never met a man who said so much without saying a word, but he dispelled that notion at once.

"C'mon in," he said, his face breaking into a warm and friendly smile.

"I don't think so," I replied.

"Why not? It's warm, it's dry, it's lively in here."

"I don't have any money with me," I said. I thought it wiser to admit to penury than apprehension, for I had never in my life been inside a bar and I wasn't used to strangers befriending me for no apparent reason.

"Money! Who needs money?" he said, seizing me by the arm and yanking me inside. "How old are you, anyhow?"

"Eighteen," I lied, adding two years to my age.

"Well, don't let that worry you. We'll just put it on my tab." He bellowed across the room at the bartender, "Two brews, George, and put it on my tab!"

I sat at the table with the bottle in my hand and tried to pour a foaming head into the cold glass, as if I were a practiced hand. I had no experience to fall back on, for in Aunt Flo's household there was no such thing as alcoholic beverages, not even watered-down wine.

"Drink up!" my friend said, and he drained off his glass in one gulp. I had never witnessed anything like it. It was as if he had unhinged something in his gullet and poured the beer down without swallowing. "A neat trick, a professional secret," he whispered to me, "but someday when I know you better I'll teach you how and you can win chug-a-lug contests hands down." He showed me the empty glass like a magician displaying an empty top hat to prove that he had actually caused the rabbit to disappear. "Now it's your turn."

I drank the full glass, the tears streaming down my face.

"Good fellow," he said, then called across the room: "George, set up two more!"

When the second round came, he said, "My name's Aaron. What's yours?"

"Just Aaron?" I asked, expecting he would supply the other half too.

"Just Aaron."

"I'm Rick," I said.

"Ah, Rick," he said, "I'm told you sailed out of the sky this afternoon and down the winds of a storm."

"Where did you hear that?"

"Why Rick, it's all the talk around here—how a boy swooped in on a blue sloop and even the captain of the *Ocean Beach Queen* had to backwater in awe."

"Were you on the ferry?"

"Was I on the ferry? Did you hear that, Henry," he said, turning to the slim, balding man who was playing the piano. "He wants to know if I was on the ferry!" Henry smiled without removing the cigarette that dangled from the corner of his mouth. He spun on his piano stool and struck a bass chord that rolled across the room. As though on cue, Aaron leaped from his chair and began to act out the episode in pantomime. First he was the enormous ferry plowing toward the wharf; then he was the irate captain in the pilot house, pulling his warn-

198

ing horn; then he was a graceful sloop, swooshing down the wind; and then he was the skipper of the sloop, a god-like boy with a wilted flower (plucked from a vase atop the piano) plaited in his tousled hair. Aaron played all the roles, his arms, legs, torso and huge head creating an epic contest that hadn't occurred quite as he depicted it but making it seem as though it had. As he performed, Henry improvised, concluding with a flourish as the blue sloop swept past the bow of the big ferry into the safety of the port.

"Another round, George!" Aaron shouted as he spun into his chair, the sweat dripping from his brow.

My lips became numb, my jaw slack. The bar filled with roisterous people, a special breed who sang, danced and flung each other gaily about. Henry relinquished his piano stool to a dumpy woman whose short legs barely reached the pedals, but who could play any song requested. Henry produced a clarinet and then somebody else pulled up a bass. As still other musicians took their places, a group gathered about to dance, clap and sing. At one point during the evening, an eldery, buxom woman with a hoarse voice, who had sung a few risque songs, poked me in the ribs.

"Sing, boy, sing!" she said. "I want to hear you sing!"

"I can't sing," I said.

"Do you hear that," she bellowed. "This boy says he can't sing!" She had baggy eyes and a heavily made up face. But she had a commanding presence and when she announced I couldn't sing, everyone in the bar began to shout, "No, no, Leona, make him sing, make him sing!"

"Who says you can't sing?" she said.

"Dora Crisp says I can't sing."

"Do you hear that!" she shouted. "Dora Crisp says he can't sing." Then to me: "Who the heck is Dora Crisp, honey?"

Before I could answer, the music started again.

Ooooooklahoma—
where the wind comes sweeping down the plain—

The clarinet, the piano, the fiddle, the voices, they were the wind and the plain. Leona put her ear near my mouth. "I want to hear you sing!"

I began to sing—a mumble, a monotone.

"Louder!" she ordered, poking me in the ribs again.

I sang a little louder.

"Belt it out, honey!" she said. "Don't be afraid! I want to hear you belt it out!"

I let loose, and my voice became a part of the swelling chorus; benumbed, my reserve gone, I was singing without worrying about pitch or key, singing out of a suppressed sense of joy.

"Do you hear that?" Leona shouted. "He says he can't sing. But listen to him sing! Did you ever hear anyone sing like that?" And she threw her arms around me and buried my head in her chest.

Aaron and I were still singing as we left Sis Norris', our voices carrying through the drizzle and the damp night air. I caught a glimpse of the black-haired girl as we passed the coffee shop, which was half-filled with customers, most of them trying to sober up after spending the night hopping from bar to bar. When we reached the ferry slip, I turned and stumbled toward my sloop and Aaron seized me by the arm.

"Where are you going?"

"To sleep," I said.

"Not there," he said. "Too risky for a man in your condition. Come with me. I'll give you a roof and bed."

"I don't know . . ." I began.

"Don't be foolish! You need a good night's sleep!"

Aaron led me to a rented room on the ground floor of a beach house halfway between the ocean and the bay. A large cast-iron bed sat in the middle of the floor and a cot against the wall. There were no windows as far as I could tell, for all four walls were covered with velvet drapes that looked like stage curtains, the way they hung.

"Here," Aaron said, "you take the bed."

I bent over to remove my sneakers and the floor began to spin. I toppled onto the soft mattress and for an instant I recalled the black-haired girl in the dirndl skirt and was consumed with a desire to get up and look for her. Then the ferry captain was waving me off and I became the defendant in a long trial in which an absent-minded judge was trying to rule on whether I had the right of way. Then Leona was poking me in the ribs, urging me to "Sing, boy sing!"

Before long I heard Aaron snoring softly. Was he asleep or play-acting again? I rose from the creaky bed, grabbed my sneakers and my slicker and stole away. I walked barefoot on the wet sidewalk to the ferry slip, where I saw the yellow light from the coffee shop reflected in pools of water on the narrow street. A drunken man was sleeping on a bench outside and the black-haired girl was serving a solitary customer within. I waited until he paid up and left, and then I went inside and sat down on a stool.

She brought me a cup of black coffee and a piece of pie. "Just for you," she said, and then she pulled a long shade down over the front door. I blew away the steam as I lifted the hot cup to my lips and an involuntary shudder of revulsion swept through my body once more.

"What's the matter?" she asked. "What happened to you, anyhow?"

When I entered the coffee shop I had no other motive except to chat with the black-haired girl and ask for something hot to drink. But now, as I gazed into her dark and sympathetic eyes, I realized I also wanted to be soothed.

"It was a horrible experience," I said, making the incident seem worse than it really was.

She leaned across the counter and kissed me on the cheek. "You're a good kid," she said. "How old are you?"

"Twenty," I said. "I turned twenty just the other day."

"You're a good kid," she said, "but you're a liar too. You're not a day over sixteen."

I looked down at my pie plate, abashed. "You're right," I said, "I'm only sixteen."

"What's you're name?"

"Rick."

"Rick," she said, "You must block this evening from your mind, forget what happened to you tonight. You must never think of it again." She was leaning toward me, rumpling my hair, whispering with intensity.

As she wiped off the counter, her indignation in-

202

creased. "Sixteen!" she said. "Can't they see you're just a boy!" She counted the money in the register, then turned out the lights, led the way outside and locked the door. She took my hand in hers as we passed the drunk still slumbering on the bench. I was wondering if she too would offer me a bed for the night, but when we reached the point of parting she turned with me toward the ferry slip.

"Where's your boat?"

"Just down here a ways."

I could see *Circe*'s mast but her hull was hidden in the swirling mist. We boarded the sloop and although we could see each other no one could see us. We stood in the cockpit, face to face, and she put her fingers to her lips and then to mine and said goodby.

10 ～

I awoke, alone, as a thin light spread across the morning sky. The rain had ceased but a dense fog shrouded the bay. The southeast wind, however, remained brisk; it was an entrenched weather wind and I knew it would be with us for another day at least before the local on-shore-offshore breezes assumed their rightful domination. I decided to chance it, to run the eight miles home by dead-reckoning. I raised my sails and set out, gauging my position by their angle to the steady breeze. I swept past black cans and red nuns as I expected, but halfway between the barrier beach and the mainland I came to know the penetrating fear of fog. There's no dread worse than the one that fills a man when he loses his bearings. Was the wind shifting without my being aware? Was I veering too far east or west where I might run aground? I assured myself it was the same reliable wind. The wind was my one verity in that blind world.

The mist was now so heavy I could barely make out the mast in front of me. All at once I saw a yellow, piercing light, perhaps a light-year away. Then the beam was on top of me, on collision course. It was from the *Miss Ocean Beach,* not the huge two-tiered ferry, but the swift rumrunner, plowing up the channel, heading right for me. To tack or jibe! I jibed, the boom crashing over and nearly taking the shrouds with it, but the sudden maneuver saved my life. The *Miss* passed astern and *Circe* rode her wake.

An hour later I saw the white rim of the sun burning through the fog. A gull passed overhead, and under its wing I saw the faint trace of shore; then the white-washed walls of a beach club loomed ahead of me, and then the mouth of the narrow Brightwaters Canal appeared, barely a hundred yards away. I had done a foolish thing; I should have waited for the fog to lift. But I had crossed the bay, guided only by my inborn sense of direction, which came from the wind.

And so way leads into way.

I told Simmy about my close encounters with the ferries, and he wrote a pithy article for the *Bay Shore Sentinel* about the rudeness of ferry captains

. . . who think they own the bay. They gun their engines while still in the harbor, they hog the channel as if it had been dredged for them alone, and they swamp smaller boats with their wakes, just because those smaller boats happen to be in their way. Why I've seen bus drivers in Manhattan who exhibit more courtesy.

It was a courageous piece, for it upbraided people Simmy knew, his own kind. I'm sure if old man Anson knew he was harboring the author of that article he would have banished him forever from his yard for antagonizing his commercial customers.

But the truth was that each year Anson hauled fewer and fewer ferries. He had been losing the big boats to his competitors, yards with more modern equipment and younger (if less colorful) hands. Anson's had become dependent upon pleasure boats that barely paid their way, and even the owners of large luxury yachts had begun to take their business elsewhere.

"It's the sheds, the wooden sheds," Simmy once confided in me. "Someday one of them sheds is going to go up like a tinderbox, just you wait and see!"

I thought I knew exactly how it would happen too. I envisioned Roy, Jr., sneaking into Oscar Boehme's work shed late at night to look for a whiskey bottle he'd hidden there. An unwitting incendiary, he would strike a match, stumble and set himself and his father's yard ablaze. Thereafter I never heard the fire whistle blow without seeing flames shooting skyward from the dried rafters at Anson's Boatyard. But the end wasn't to come in quite that way. Old man Anson wasn't done in by a roaring fire, but by diminishing capital.

I took Simmy's article to the *Sentinel* office after supper. It was one of those balmy evenings in which the fading onshore breeze wafted up the long, straight streets that led to the bay, rustling the leaves in the stately maples. The *Sentinel* was located north of Main Street in a narrow, two-story building with a steeply pitched roof. This structure, with its exposed timbers over a stucco facade and twin bowed windows that framed a stone stoop, looked as if it belonged in Shakespeare's England. The Elizabethan replica seemed perfectly apt, however, for a county that bore the name of Suffolk and had been settled by seventeenth-century whaling men.

I didn't climb the front stoop. Instead I cut through a parking lot to the one-story plant out back that housed the printing press. Even before I entered I could hear the rattle of the linotype machines and feel their consuming heat. It was more than youthful caprice that lured me to this unlovely place, so noisy and infernally hot.

Seven weekly newspapers, blanketing Suffolk County, were printed in that plant. All seven were owned by the wealthy congressman, W. Kingsland Macy, whose picture appeared regularly amid their pages, high starched Hoover collar and all. And so these newspapers weren't really newspapers; they were organs for the promulgation of Macy's political ideals. But, at sixteen, I had no interest in politics and no use for ideals.

I was interested in the linotype operators, bathed in sweat, their fingers gliding across the keys; in the hot lead that dropped from their machines into metal trays; in the compositors who arranged those lines of type in iron chases, which they locked with a special key. One of them spread a damp sheet of newsprint over an inked chase and, with a wooden mallet, pounded out a page proof for an anxious editor. The sound of the mallet against the chase reminded me of the echo of the caulking hammer across the shipyard. When the editor approved the proof, two men carried the chase to the flat-bed press and placed it beside other chases, each one a page.

After a while I heard the rumble of the flat-bed press.

A roll of newsprint, mounted on a giant spindle, began to turn. A continuous stream of paper twisted over the chases, as intricate as a cat's cradle or a spider's web. Enormous rollers depressed the flowing stream of newsprint against the hardened type. Eventually a 32-page newspaper dropped down a chute into a bin, each sheet printed on both sides, properly inserted and neatly trimmed. A waiting driver tied the newspapers into bundles and loaded them on his truck.

I walked along a narrow corridor, passed the proofreading cubicles and into the editorial room. A halfdozen men were there, some talking, some typing and some sitting idly with their feet up on their desks. I glanced into the familiar corner where Vic Scanlon could usually be found, but he wasn't there. So I went to the entrance and sat on the stoop, waiting for him to arrive.

The *Sentinel* office was situated across the street from the elementary school. Behind the school a softball game was in progress between two teams in the community league. I couldn't see the diamond, but I could hear the cheering voices of the spectators and the occasional dull thud of bat against ball. Shortly thereafter I saw Vic scurrying around the building and across the front lawn, carrying a bunch of scorecards in his hand.

He was a heavy-set man of about five feet six, nearly as wide as he was tall. But for all his heft he was never still. He moved constantly—he had to. Scanlon had become a sports writer for the *Sentinel* while he was still in high school and he had joined the editorial staff right after graduation in the heart of the great Depression a decade earlier. He had never worked anywhere else. Now, in his mid-thirties, he had six children and he supported them by hustling. In addition to being editor of the *Sentinel,* the largest paper in the Macy chain, he was the Suffolk sports editor for *The Long Island Press,* a stringer for *The New York Times,* a publicist for the local Republican party, a sometime speech writer for Macy, and the editor of a "throwaway" filled with Italian recipes and published by a grocery chain. To the best of my knowledge, the charge of "conflict of interest" never arose, and if it had Scanlon's children would have starved. On the contrary, he was widely admired for his doggedness. Vic never earned much at any job, but he made up for it by having lots of them.

With it all, he was a cheerful man with a strong streak of generosity. He never bought one can of beer, but always two—one for himself and one for a friend who happened along. He couldn't walk a block without running into half-a-dozen people he knew—or who knew him. But he didn't know Jolly Beane.

"Okay Rick," he said as he came up to the stoop, "who's our friend lambasting today?"

I handed him Simmy's piece about ferry captains and he whistled through his teeth. When he finished reading, he reached into his wallet and handed me five dollars. One of the things I liked most about Vic was that he never pumped me to find out Jolly Beane's true identity. I think for a while he thought I was Beane, but I assured him my sole contribution was the punctuation, not the words.

"Well," he had said to me, "commas, periods, semicolons—they're words, too, of a kind. Use them well."

Just as we were about to part, the fire whistle blew, and the recurrent fleeting image of Anson's going up in smoke swept through my mind. The firehouse was around the corner from the *Sentinel,* and the blare had hardly faded in the night air when a fire truck shot past the *Sentinel* office, volunteers in shirt-sleeves hanging off the sides, and came to an abrupt halt about a block away. Vic shoved a pad and pencil into my hand. "Hurry up," he said, "run over there and find out what's going on!"

I raced to the scene, hoping for a three-alarm conflagration at least, but it was over before I arrived. Two volunteers were chatting amiably with the proprietor of the gas station about the softball game when I strode up to them, full of purpose.

"I'm from the *Sentinel,*" I said. "What happened here?"

They told me the back seat of a nearby car had caught on fire, apparently the result of a carelessly thrown cigarette. The gas station attendant noticed the smoke while he was filling the tank. He jumped into the car, drove it away from his pumps, and called the fire department. The only damage was to the upholstery in the back seat.

When I returned to the *Sentinel* with this information, Vic pushed me into a chair in front of a typewriter, as if I had been witness to the most hair-raising event in the history of Bay Shore. "Here," he said, "write it all out! Tell me what you know."

I stared at the blank piece of paper in the typewriter for a long time, wondering what to put down. I didn't want to disappoint Vic; I felt he wanted me to make something out of my experience, forge it into a tale. Gradually a sentence formed in my head and I wrote:

A major explosion was narrowly averted this evening when a quick-thinking gasoline station attendant leaped into a burning car and drove it away from his fuel tanks.

Then I typed out several more paragraphs, supplying the remaining details. When Vic read the story, a broad smile spread across his face. "Punctuation is pretty good," he said. When the next edition of the *Sentinel* appeared, my story was on the bottom of the front page.

Vic didn't pay me for that effort, but he did something better. He gave me my first by-line.

The *Bay Shore Sentinel* no longer exists and Vic Scanlon is dead, but in those days, in Scanlon's newspaper, a major explosion—even one that was "narrowly averted" —was considered newsworthy.

To find a friend isn't hard; it's impossible. We don't find friends. Lives cross and by chance a friendship flares. It's only later that we say, "I found a friend," as if we had been seeking that specific person all along.

In truth, I wasn't even looking for a friend. I was looking for someone who could tend my jib sheets properly, for I had it in the back of my mind that I might race *Circe* after all. I invited a number of acquaintances to try their hand at it, but not one had the patience or timing to do it well. When coming about, they would either let the jib sheet luff too soon or trim it too soon, killing our headway. Most of my "would-be" friends didn't want to tend the jib; they wanted to take the helm and leave the sheets to me. And so they really weren't my friends at all.

211

It wasn't until the following summer that I found someone who could sail with me. His name was Martin Newcomb and our relationship began on an auspicious August afternoon. I was sailing toward my mooring in a dying breeze after a brisk sail, when a procession of cars went by on the road parallel to the canal, blaring their horns. I thought they were part of a wedding party until the fire whistle went off and then horns, sirens and firecrackers filled the air.

As I drifted past a jetty, I saw Martin standing on the edge, more interested in my sloop than the din. I knew him slightly; I had seen him wandering forlornly up and down the canal, looking at the boats as if he were hoping something might turn up to brighten his days. I had wanted to talk to him—and now I did.

"What's going on? Sounds like the Fourth of July."

"Haven't you heard?"

"No. I've been sailing all afternoon."

"The war's over," he said.

The war had been a backdrop to my youth, as the Depression had been to my boyhood, bringing rationing and scarcity, distant destruction and death. Two of my classmates had brothers who were killed in action and another had a brother who was a prisoner of war. The war had never touched me directly; I hadn't been bombed or lost a close relative, or seen people die. Yet it was always present, like a lethal gas, and I could never entirely escape the oppressive feeling of futility and loss. Now with its end, I had this illusion that I would be liberated and my world would change, and in that moment of joy I wanted to reach out and touch a friend.

But I had been warned about befriending Martin

212

Newcomb by no less a judge of character than Neil Oden, who was still trying to master his brother's dinghy. Now and then he would telephone me with advice about how to improve the sailability of my sloop. He had become an authority on how to rake a mast, and he would tell me I could "point much higher" if I would only tighten my aft stay. He had also been studying hydrodynamics and lectured me about Bernoulli's Equation until I told him I knew all about Bernoulli since I took high school physics too. However, it had never occurred to me that anything I learned in physics had anything to do with sailing a boat.

I knew what Oden wanted, of course. He wanted an invitation, and he had no compunction about reminding me that I had sailed with him when I had no boat of my own. That was true—and beside the point. In Neil Oden I hadn't found a true friend. I made excuses; I put him off. I couldn't bring myself to let a plumber like Oden aboard *Circe*. To do so struck me as an act of profanity.

When all else failed, Neil tried to build himself up by bad-mouthing others. "You know that guy, Newcomb," he said to me one day.

"I've seen him around."

"Stay away from him. Boy, is he dumb!"

"Is he?"

"He doesn't even live here—just comes for summers and stays with his grandparents."

"What's the matter with that?"

"What's the matter with that? As soon as you meet him he starts to tell you about how his grandfather founded the incorporated village of Brightwaters, about how his **grandfather** owns half the stock in the Pennsylvania

213

Railroad, about how his grandfather did this and did that."

"Well, maybe his grandfather did do all those things. If I had a grandfather who did all those things, I might boast about him too."

"That's not it. He's only trying to impress you because he wants you to feel honored to invite him aboard your boat. I'll bet he doesn't even know how to sail!"

I figured a bad reference from Neil Oden was tantamount to a good reference from anybody else.

When I reached my mooring post, Martin was standing on the shore and I tossed him my stern line. He pulled the sloop slowly toward shore, fending off the stern, and then he dropped a clove hitch around a post in the bulkhead and coiled the rest of the line. We chatted while I removed the sails. I expected him to start telling me how his grandfather founded the village and owned half the Pennsylvania Railroad, but he never said a word about those things. Instead he talked about the boats in the canal, how many nice ones there were, and how he thought my sloop was the prettiest of them all. When I started ashore with an empty bucket, he said: "I'll fill it for you, if you want." I handed the bucket to him and watched him out of the corner of my eye as he filled it and carried it back, leaning against its weight. He was small, lean and nearsighted, and he squinted all the time, even with his glasses on.

The salt was streaked across my varnished deck. I splashed the fresh water on the surface and washed it down while Martin went for a second bucket. When I finished, I asked, "Do you sail?"

"A little," he said. "Mostly down on the Jersey shore.

214

That's where I live. We have Barnegat Bay sneakboxes down there. Ever hear of them?"

I said I had seen pictures of them, and then I added, "Would you like to sail with me?"

"You bet I would," he said. "You bet I would."

"If you're free around ten tomorrow," I said, "meet me here. That's about the time I like to raise my sails."

He was there, waiting for me, as I knew he would be. I pulled my jib out of the sailbag and dropped it on the deck. He examined it silently, testing the snaps and the batten pockets for tears as he slipped the battens in. He attached the jib to the forestay and tied the clew to the jib sheet without instructions from me. When he finished, he helped me with the mainsail, steadying the cradle, pulling the outhaul, attaching the halyard to the sail-head. He was quick and accurate, and we moved in unison without getting in each other's way.

"Did you ever hear of Bernoulli's Equation?" I asked.

"Of what?" he said.

"Bernoulli's Principle," I said, sounding now like Neil Oden. "You know, the faster the wind moves across the back of the mainsail, the less the pressure. That, and the keel, are what drive the sloop forward."

"You must be kidding," he said. "I don't know anything about that."

"Neither did I," I said, "until this character who can't sail worth a darn told me about it the other day."

"Whose principle?" Martin asked, squinting into the sun, studying the pennant atop my mast.

"Never mind," I said.

We raised the mainsail. Martin stood on the deck beside the mast and pulled down on the main halyard, hand over hand, while I gathered up the slack under the cuddy. When the sail appeared to be as high as it would go, he seized the halyard about a foot over his head and lifted himself off the deck, raising it another inch or so. The mainsail had never set so well before or the boom hung so high.

We raised the jib in the same manner, and then Martin pulled the sloop slowly to the mooring post and draped my painter over the top. Then he held the clew of the jib in his hand and backwinded the sail until it caught a puff and headed us in the direction we wanted to go. As our sails filled, Martin scurried across the deck to the cockpit and trimmed the sheets. *Circe* heeled and slanted across the canal. Midway across we caught a clear wind and pointed high. A half-dozen crisp tacks and we were free, beyond the last breakwater, cutting the waves and catching the spray. Martin let out a whoop, and I did too, for his unexpected expression of exhilaration was contagious. We practiced tacking, and in a short time we had it down pat, as if we'd been sailing together all our lives.

"Ready-about!" I would say, and Martin would squat on the lee side under the boom, poised like a cat.

"Hard-a-lee!"—and I would swing the bow into the wind. Just before the jib luffed, Martin would free the sheet. The instant the bow crossed the wind, he'd trim the other sheet, firm and tight, and we'd be pointing high on the opposite tack with little loss of headway. For a while we would sail upwind. I'd sit on the lee side of the cockpit, watching the jib, and he would sprawl prone on the windward deck, which seemed to have been designed with his small frame in mind. Every now and then he would glance back at me, his glasses fogged.

Later on, we practiced jibing, and then we sailed with the wind behind. Martin set my whisker pole, something I could never do when I sailed alone, and we glided easily, wing-and-wing. A daring thought crossed my mind.

"Let's fly the spinnaker!"

Martin looked at me skeptically. "Do you know how to set it?"

"Sure," I said. "Don't you?"

"Sure," he said. "Let's go!"

In my two seasons of sailing *Circe* I had never once raised her spinnaker because it takes two to fly the big sail and, in a stiff blow, three. But I always carried the spinnaker pole, mounted on brackets under the cuddy, and I always brought the big sail aboard—just in case the opportunity arose.

Neither of us had ever set a spinnaker, and neither of us was about to let on. We improvised as we went along. Martin attached the spinnaker halyard to the peak of the sail and hoisted it. I secured the sheet on the leeward side far aft—so far so good. The big sail was up there, fluttering crazily, but it wouldn't fill with wind.

Martin clambered out on the foredeck with the spinnaker boom, which was twice as long as he. He was like a puny pole vaulter with no room to move. Somehow he managed to snap the end of the pole into the windward edge of the sail, but it was while he was trying to secure the other end of boom to the mast that the situation got out of control. I leaned forward and gave the guy a tug and the big sail billowed, exerting tremendous forward pressure on the unsecured pole. Martin was inching up the deck, hanging onto the pole for dear life.

"Let it go! Let it go!" I shouted.

"Head up! Head up!" he replied.

The next thing I knew Martin was no longer on the deck; he was soaring through the air, arms outstretched, a beautiful swan dive. He splashed down forty feet away.

Now I did head up, and Martin swam toward me, sputtering and cussing the whole way. I helped him back on board and he sat on the deck, blinking and dripping —and then we both began to laugh crazily, tears streaming down our face, while the loose spinnaker twisted around the forestay.

That night Martin and I went to the library to see if we could find a text that showed us how to fly a spinnaker without falling overboard. We found nothing helpful.

"Why don't we ask somebody who knows how?" Martin said.

"Come on," I said. "I know who!"

I found Schuyler Hubbard sitting on his porch, listening to his radio.

"Some sailors pull the spinnaker right out of the sail bag, or a special box that sets up there on the deck," he said, "but I always found that to be a nuisance. In my day, we tied the spinnaker up in "stops" to keep it from filling too soon. Get yourself some yarn and wrap it around the spinnaker in five or six places. Make sure the bottom one is the tightest—the higher you go, the looser the yarn. Then when you've got sheets and guy and boom all set, cut the bottom "stop" and let the wind blow out the others until she fills."

As we walked home, Martin kept saying: "It sounds so simple, so deceptively simple."

It took some practice, though—to tie those strands of yarn just right, not too loose and not too tight. But we finally mastered it, and one day sailed downwind on a brisk southwester, the spinnaker billowing ahead, the water boiling behind, until we thought we would rise right out of the following waves and take to the sky.

I would rather have sailed alone than with someone who broke the spell of the moving sloop by chattering away; Martin and I could sail for hours without breaking our covenant of silence. Once ashore, however, Martin jabbered away about racing.

"We're a fantastic team! We can out-sail anyone! I know we can!"

"Maybe yes," I said, "and maybe no." I was thinking of the grueling high school football season, followed by basketball and then baseball—the year-long competition, the pressure to win or, perhaps more accurately, stave off defeat. Summer was a time of respite from all that; besides, I never regarded sailing as a competitive sport. To sail a sloop was akin to writing a poem, or at least to reading one.

As I grew older, it struck me that what I sought in sailing wasn't victory over others, or even over myself, but atonement, a reconciliation with the gods. In one of her rare moments of insight, Aunt Flo had told me that atonement really meant "at-one-ment," to be at "one" with God. God, to me, meant the gods of the wind, the sun, the moon and the tides, and grace meant to have achieved a state of unification with them.

For a long time I thought that when Aunt Flo referred

to God she was talking about the God we beseeched and whose name we took in vain, the white-haired authoritarian figure who dwelt in the skies. But I was wrong, for God, to Aunt Flo, was a pervasive spirit who inhabited all space and the human soul. Was her pervasive God much different from my pagan gods? I didn't think so.

The only difference was that Aunt Flo's God was a symbol of abstract love. I don't know if she meant it that way, but the love she preached never quite came down off its pedestal. For me love couldn't be quite so pure; it must contain passion, affection, even jealousy. It would have to include a human embrace. There were times when it needed to glow gently and other times when it should sear. Love would have to be an "at-one-ment" too.

I hadn't yet found that kind of love, but I believed some day if I were vigilant it would come to me. I wouldn't be deprived. But I already knew enough about myself to realize I couldn't reach out and seize the day. I didn't think anyone could, for life didn't operate that way. I had to sail roundabout, to tack, to jibe, to wait for a favorable wind, to make the best of the breeze I had. Patience, persistence, faith in the ultimate kindliness of the elements—that's where deliverance lay.

And so it seemed a sacrilege to employ the winds and tides to assert a flimsy superiority. That's not what the winds and tides were for. Winds and tides were the elements the gods supplied to take me where I had to go.

And yet . . . and yet it is difficult to deny the imp of perversity. The desire to compete ran so strongly within Martin Newcomb that it infected me. I began to taste the heady grape of victory. If competition was contrary to my nature it was consonant with his. Since that was the case, what right had I to stand in my friend's way? I waited for Martin to broach the subject again, and when he did I said with exasperation, as though he had worn me down, "All right, all right, we'll race her. But not this year. Next spring we'll scrape her bottom down to bare wood and sand her fine. Meanwhile we'll read up on the racing rules."

"Starboard tack," Martin said. "The close-hauled boat on the starboard tack has the right of way. That's all you need to know."

"We'll have to practice starts," I said.

"Yeah, starts! The gun goes off! Two seconds later we cross the starting line! Bam!" He slammed the fist of one hand into the palm of the other.

"But it takes timing to do that! Cross the line before the gun . . ."

"Never! We'd never do anything as dumb as that!"

"Then after you cross the starting line, what do you do?"

"Fly to windward! Clear the fleet and fly to windward!"

"But what if we miscalculate? What if we cross the line last and we've got the whole fleet zigging and zagging all around us?"

"No, no, you don't understand! You don't do it that way!"

All that winter Martin and I exchanged letters filled with information about how to start, how to round a mark, how to cover a competitor on an upwind leg, and how to keep another boat from getting an "overlap" on a downwind leg. It was no use trying to tell myself the excitement was artificially induced. I dreamed about

Race Week, and in my visions *Circe* was named Queen of the Bay.

I was now in my final year of high school and I knew the summer ahead would be a watershed, an interlude, the last idyll of my youth before going off to college, and it seemed fitting that I should spend it testing myself against others. I was convinced that after this summer my life would never be the same again. Ahead I saw nothing but the encumbrances of responsibility; I felt the dread of that word "duty" which Aunt Flo had drummed into my head.

Martin showed up in late June and we picked up where we had left off the summer before. Race Week wasn't until the first week in August and so we had ample time to tune up. We joined the Islip Boat Club, which held handicap races every weekend, and it was there we began to sail against the old man in the straw hat with his two grandchildren as crew.

Our first race was scheduled for a Saturday—the warning gun to go off at 1 P.M. I didn't sleep the night before. Martin and I raised sails at 11 A.M., giving us a full two hours to sail the mile and a half to the starting line off Bayberry Point. The wind was light out of the northwest, barely a wind at all, and in the long canal there wasn't a trace of breeze. We began to paddle; then Martin pulled the boat along the shore while I steered. Just as the fire whistle sounded its noon blast we reached the open bay.

"There's still plenty of time," Martin said. "We'll make it. There's bound to be a breeze."

We would glide for about a hundred yards on a gentle puff, then lay hot and lazy, and then glide some more. We

222

were still 20 minutes from the starting line when we heard the warning gun. The committee boat, a cabin cruiser owned by one Captain Plunkett (a retired tugboat captain who served as the Club commodore for his own amusement) was anchored on the still water about a mile away. He might as well have been halfway around the earth. An imaginary line from the bow of the cruiser to a drooping flag in the center of an anchored rowboat formed the starting line. About thirty boats were drifting on both sides of the line, including the robin's-egg blue Timber Point with the familiar figure at the helm.

"How come they all got out here on time while we're still drifting around?" Martin said. "They must have started out at the crack of dawn!" Only later did we learn that Captain Plunkett had assured himself of a quorum by sailing up and down all the creeks in his cruiser, collecting the sloops of stalwart members and towing them out to the starting line. He was going to have his race, even if it was a drifting match.

Captain Plunkett had raised a blue flag to indicate the course he wanted us to sail. It was a triangular course with the first leg a beat to windward into the dying breeze. He had divided the fleet into two sections; the larger boats including the Timber Points would start first with the smaller ones, like the Snipes and Comets, to follow. The winner of each section would be adjudged on corrected time—but there was always the thrill of finishing first.

When the starting gun went off, we still had about a quarter-mile to reach the starting line. Most of the sloops were laying right on the line, waiting for a puff. It came, lasting about 20 seconds, and the boats went off in different directions. I noted the old man with the straw hat pointed due north, toward the mainland.

"I think he's making a mistake," Martin said.

"So do I. So do I."

We were of the same mind—the fading northwest wind wouldn't last. When it died, a fresh wind would spring up from the southwest, and so the best tactic would be to sail not toward the north but toward the south.

We reached the starting line, long after everyone else, in a dead calm. The sloops with the most wind had tacked to the north, but they would be out of position when the shift came—if it came. And it did come, just as we crossed the starting line. We saw it rippling across the water, reflecting the light from the high-riding sun. "Here it comes, here it comes," Martin whispered, as if he were afraid he might give our shared secret away.

The wind hit our sails and *Circe* heeled. Martin trimmed the sheet slightly for a close reach and we were off, sailing toward the first marker on a windward leg that was a windward leg no more. I looked for the old man under his straw hat, and I saw his Timber Point hugging the mainland, sailing the old wind. He appeared unperturbed, as though he would be happy to sail that same wind through all eternity. It seemed so strange; we were barely a mile apart, yet the old man was sailing a dying wind from the north while we were sailing a rising wind from the south.

Then the old man's sails luffed gently, and all at once he was surrounded by the new wind and had to alter the setting of his sails and change his course. He was still closer to the first marker than we were as the crow flies, but he wasn't a crow. He had to tack while all we had to do was to sail a straight line. We had been favored by the gods; by arriving late we had gained the upper hand. We rounded the first marker ahead of the fleet and we never relinquished our lead. As we crossed the finish line, Captain Plunkett fired a blank and Martin danced on the deck.

"We did it!" he said. "I told you we could do it!"

"Luck," I said, "it was luck!"

"Luck, nothing! We knew what we were doing and they didn't."

I came about and headed for the committee boat. The old man, who had finally crossed the finish line, passed us sailing the other way, going home. He waved graciously, and his grandchildren looked at us curiously, as if they were hardly aware they had been in a race.

As we sailed by the committee boat, I saw Captain Plunkett standing on the bow with his pot belly protruding over his belt and his steel-rimmed glasses sliding down his nose.

"Nice race," he hollered rather begrudgingly, as if it weren't quite right to join a club and then beat all the stalwarts in my first outing.

"Say," I called back, "who's the fellow in the other Timber Point?"

"That's Frank Gulden," he replied.

"Who?"

"Gulden, Gulden! You know, the mustard tycoon!"

"Some tycoon," Martin said as we sailed away. "How can he be a tycoon when he can't even anticipate a change in the wind?"

The ways of the rich baffled me. I was intrigued by their wealth and intimidated by their power. In their presence I was deferential: because they had money, I assumed, they were better than I was. But now, after my victory over the mustard tycoon, I saw that money didn't endow a man with special qualities. For he'd proved just as fallible and just as human as anyone else. At least in this instance.

Race Week also caused me to see how too much money and leisure can addle men's minds.

There were only three Timber Points entered in the traditional regatta off Great River, including *Circe*. Rather than have these three contend against each other, the race committee put us into the handicap class where we had to vie with the largest, swiftest sloops on the bay. The winner of each race would be determined on corrected time, and so we were really racing against the clock and not each other. But time is intangible, an illusion. In the heat of competition it's hard to remember that the enemy isn't the sloop to windward but the unseen seconds ticking away.

There were nine boats entered in the handicap class, including the renowned *Apache*, which for years running had been selected by the redoubtable members of the race committee as Queen of the Bay. *Queen of the Bay*— that was a laurel *Apache* literally owned. I thought we might wrest the title from her, but when I saw her for the first time I was filled with despair. She was a sleek, 30-foot beauty. Instead of an ordinary cuddy like *Circe*'s, she had a bubble-turret molded of plexiglass that offered almost no resistance to the wind. She flew an enormous genoa jib, trimmed well aft, which funneled the wind past the back of the mainsail, thus lowering the pressure and increasing the lift. And her long hull knifed through the water like the dorsal fin of a shark.

Martin and I came upon her unexpectedly as we cruised toward Great River the day before the regatta began. She glided out of the east, swung up to the stern of a waiting launch, luffed, lowered her vast sails, and was towed off to a snug and secret harbor somewhere, not to materialize again until shortly before race time.

"That's her," I said to Martin.

"I see! I see," he said petulantly, as if he wished I had pretended she wasn't there, as if she were a phantom or a mirage. But she was all too real!

"What do you see?"

"I see a sloop, like any other sloop," he said.

"Then you're blind."

"What do you see?" he asked.

"I see the Queen of the Bay," I said. I was cowed before we began. I was ready to come about on the spot and return home.

"I'll grant you," he said, "that she does sail a mite faster than *Circe*. But so what!"

"She points higher too. Did you see how close she headed into the wind?"

"What do you expect. She's half again as long as us along the waterline and she carries nearly twice the sail."

"We don't stand a chance against her," I said.

"Listen," Martin said, "you're not sailing against *Apache*. You're sailing against the skipper of that boat, and you can sail as well as he can, any day."

I knew then that I would never have a more loyal friend, but I also knew that Martin was mistaken. I

227

wasn't daunted by *Apache* as much as by her swarthy skipper, Duncan Cawley. There were those who swore Cawley was half Highland Scot and others who claimed he was half Mohawk Indian. Both tales were unfounded, and both grew out of the man's legendary ferocity. When challenged, it was said, he would ram an opponent's vessel rather than give way.

Cawley was the unmannered playboy of the Great South Bay, and the sole heir of a dowager aunt who owned a string of department stores. As a boy, I supposed, she had bought him toys and as a man she bought him boats, which he stripped and rebuilt to his own rugged taste. Captain Hubbard had told me about Duncan Cawley.

"He's some mechanic, that man is," the captain had said. To be called a "mechanic" by Schuyler Hubbard was high tribute from a man who was spare with his praise.

Cawley owned a lapstraked fishing skiff that he sailed through the breakers, barely a hundred yards offshore, on stormy days—to the consternation of the Coast Guard; and he owned *Apache*, Queen of the Bay, which he rigged (again according to local legend) only for major regattas and minor gales. The winds that tempted him made me thankful I had sense enough to stay ashore. So I knew Martin was wrong; I couldn't have sailed as well as Duncan Cawley, even if I had a dowager aunt who indulged my whims.

And yet, after two days of racing against Cawley, I began to tell myself that maybe I was wrong. In each of those two races I steeled myself to sail against the clock, as if *Apache* weren't there. It was a sound tactic, one not to be abandoned without good cause. Out of nine boats in our class, we had taken a fourth on the first day and a second the next day and, although *Apache* had two firsts, she still wasn't that much ahead on corrected time.

After the second race, as we sailed into our berth in Great River, I announced: "A first in the third race, and another in the fourth race. That's what we need."

"Keep sailing the way you are," Martin said. "Don't worry about *Apache*. Don't worry about anybody else. Just sail each race the best you can."

To sail my kind of race, however, I'd need my kind of wind, and I was concerned about the lowering sky. For two days we'd had steady southwesterly winds, but now, to the west, a new weather system was moving in and dark rain clouds stretched across the sky. We pulled into a mooring amid thirty or forty other boats, all tied together to form a giant raft. Race Week was like that—one big happy carnival with boat owners tramping back and forth across each other's decks, sleeping aboard, and carousing until dawn. For most skippers, it wasn't the sailing that lured them as much as the festivities, a chance to remove their normal ballast and replace it with bottles of gin.

Martin and I had just lowered our sails when the committee boat, a 40-foot-long twin-powered diesel came steaming down the river full blast, raising a huge wake. It was precisely the sort of imbecility that would have inspired Simm Wicks to write a vituperative article for the *Sentinel* about the helmsmanship of wealthy yachtsmen with their carpeted cabins and portholes with venetian blinds. The vessel ran by the flotilla once, raising a series of waves that dashed the sailboats

229

against each other and flipped one tipsy sailor overboard; then it doubled back and stirred up a second series of waves. Angry skippers were waving the yacht off, but Horace Ralston—senior member of a Wall Street brokerage house, chairman of the regatta, and the big boat's proud owner—was entirely oblivious to the commotion. He was on an errand of mercy, dressed in a blue blazer, white flannels ducks and white buck shoes. Standing in the stern with a bullhorn around his neck, Ralston raised his hand and his captain threw the boat into reverse and backed up to the flotilla. Putting the bullhorn to his mouth, he announced that a storm was on its way (as anyone could see) and that "all ships were advised to secure themselves accordingly and take proper precautions!" Meanwhile he was causing more havoc with his wake than the storm was likely to cause with its waves.

Satisfied that he had saved the fleet, Ralston put his bullhorn down as Martin shouted, his voice carrying on the wind: "You blithering idiot, get your bloody bus out of here!"

"What?" Ralston asked.

"You heard me," Martin hollered. "Get your stupid bus out of here!" He had climbed up on the stern and was hanging out from a stay defiantly. Meanwhile I retreated to the cuddy and tried to make myself as small as possible.

Ralston ordered his yacht backed up to *Circe* and, looking severely at Martin asked, "Young man, what's your name?"

"What's yours?" Martin replied.

Ralston was apoplectic. "Young man, my name is Horace Ralston and, for your information, I'm the chairman of this regatta!"

"And my name is Martin Newcomb the Third and, for your information, my grandfather owns half the Pennsylvania Railroad!"

Ralston sputtered and spewed and sped off, raising another great wake, as a cheer rose from the sailors of the battered flotilla who had overhead the entire exchange.

The drenching rains fell, chilling all hands, filling the bilges, collecting in pools and running in rivulets down the decks and through the scuppers into the bay. The storm blew past at dawn, but in its wake left a gusty northeaster that turned early August into late October. The wind blew at gale force from the mainland to the sea, contravening the laws of nature. In such a wind it wasn't possible to sail under full canvas; so Martin and I took a reef in the mainsail and prayed that Ralston and his committee had sense enough to cancel that day's race.

But the race committee, in its infinite wisdom, chose to set a three-legged course, just as if it were another balmy day on the Great South Bay. The committee did, however, make one concession to the elements: instead of the usual upwind beat, the first leg would be a short run with the wind astern. Their thinking, we supposed, was that this would lead to less cut-throat maneuvering around the starting line; but they failed to take into account the savage delights of Duncan Cawley.

Since the swiftest sloops were in the handicap class, we were scheduled to start first. The other classes would follow at three minute intervals: Stars, the true racing machines, customarily sailed by the most ossified skippers; Narrasketucks, a budding new class of flat-bottomed boats with planing hulls that often overtook the Stars on a downwind leg, and Lightnings. These would go around the five-mile course twice. The smaller sloops —Snipes, Cape Cods, Comets, and tiny gaff-rigged SS boats—would go around once. Most of them were to capsize before the race even began.

The thrill of racing occurs in those tense minutes before the starting gun as the boats jockey for position along the starting line. The objective is to cross that line just as soon as possible after the gun goes off and as close as possible to the windward end of the line. Cross too soon and you must start all over again. Cross too far to leeward and you're blanketed by the sails of every other boat and must tack to clear your wind.

I had observed Cawley closely on previous starts and noticed how he loved to sail straight up the starting line before the gun, as if he owned it, intimidating everyone else, even those who had the right away. He had no compunctions about crowding or hurling epithets or shaking his fist at anyone who dared try to cross his bow. I had ignored his bold tactics, timing my own start in my own way while Martin counted off the seconds from a stop watch he held in his hand. But now I was afraid that if I let *Apache* get too far ahead of me in this stiff wind I would never make up for lost time. When I saw Cawley barge up the starting line, I followed him, barely a boat length behind. When he veered, I veered; when he tacked, I tacked; when he jibed, I jibed. I was his shadow and he led me a merry chase, but he couldn't shake me.

"For heaven's sake!" Martin shouted at me. "Let him

go! Sail your own race! You can't beat him this way!"

But I was determined to stay on his tail. I was transfixed by this demonic man who was sailing bare-chested despite the chill, with a headband around his curly red hair.

Thirty seconds before the gun he veered to the wrong side of the starting line, hoping to strand me there; but when he veered back to the right side of the line, I was still on his stern. Next he luffed and came about, and then—perhaps five seconds before the gun—he yanked his tiller to windward, let out his sails and shot for the starting line with *Circe* right behind. The gun sounded an instant before he crossed and he let out a wild banshee scream that seemed to come more out of the spirit of the howling wind than the mouth of a man. It was a practiced, primitive cry intended to distract us, but we didn't lose our nerve.

I was sure I could stay off *Apache*'s stern twice around the course, and I was determined not to let Cawley slip free. Though I tried to block his wind from behind, it was no use; *Apache* was too swift. With every hundred yards we sailed, *Apache* gained ten on *Circe*. Still, as we approached the first mark, a black can which we had to jibe, Cawley wasn't that far away.

"We can't lose time around this mark!" I shouted. "If we do, he'll be gone!"

"Don't jibe!" Martin warned. "It's too windy. Come about the long way!"

"Stand ready to jibe!" I ordered.

I saw *Apache* jibe ahead of me; Cawley went around the mark without hesitation and *Apache* responded to his skill.

233

"Don't jibe!" Martin warned again. Then, seeing I couldn't be swayed, he began to trim the mainsail with alacrity as we came up to the mark. I pushed the tiller with all my strength against the weather helm; the boom came crashing across the deck and *Circe* skewered out of control. She headed off the wind, then up the wind, then off the wind. I tried to steer but the tiller only jiggled about loosely.

"What's the matter?" Martin said. "Get her going! What are you doing anyhow?"

The Stars had now caught up to us and their skippers were furiously waving me out of the way. One by one they jibed the mark, and one by one their masts cracked and their white sails came tumbling down.

Gradually I realized what had happened to *Circe*. Luckily we hadn't cracked our mast, but we had lost our rudder. The pressure of the water against the rudder was evidently too great as we jibed. Perhaps a fitting had been loose. Whatever the reason, my rudder was now floating off somewhere and we were out of control. We were one of a half-dozen sloops floundering about the black can—and now far away to the west, all by herself, was the Queen of the Bay.

"That's that!" Martin said with finality, as I glanced across the water to see a launch from the committee boat approaching us with Ralston and his bullhorn standing in the stern.

"Do you see what I see?" I said to Martin.

"Yeah, I see," Martin said. "Watch, he's going to tell us we're disqualified."

"Are you all right there, Newcomb?" Ralston inquired over his bullhorn.

234

"Yes sir," Martin shouted. "We just lost a rudder. That's all."

The launch retrieved us first. Ralston tossed a line to Martin and then grabbed our hands to steady us as we leaped aboard the launch. The other sloops tied up in tandem behind *Circe* and their skippers remained aboard while being towed.

As we headed back to Great River, where Ralston had suffered Martin's insolence only the evening before, I expected a stern reprimand at the very least, but all Ralston kept saying was, "Oops, there goes another one," each time another jibing sloop lost its mast around the fateful can. He said it like a disinterested observer watching toothpicks snap. Then, as we entered the protected waters of the river, Ralston turned to Martin and said: "So Marty Newcomb is your grandad?"

"Yes sir, he is."

"Well, give him my regards, will you?"

"Yes sir, I will."

"Your Grandad and I—we did some pretty fair horse-trading in our day. Yes indeed. Did your Grandad ever tell you about the time we cornered the market in sunflower seeds?"

"No sir, he never told me that one."

Ralston chuckled. "Well, next time you see him, ask him to tell you about the time he and Harry Ralston cornered the market in sunflower seeds."

As we neared the sheltered shore, Ralston turned to me for the first time. "Well, young man," he said, "I trust you learned something about racing this afternoon."

"Yes sir," I said. "I sure did."

We boarded our sloop again and Ralston cut us loose.

"Tell me, young man, just what did you learn today?" Martin asked in a stentorian voice after the launch had disappeared.

"I learned, sir, never to jibe a mark in a high wind, no matter what the stakes."

Oscar Boehme built a new rudder for *Circe,* and by the following weekend we were out again, competing against the sloops of the Islip Boat Club where a measure of sanity could be found. These races were pleasant interludes against congenial skippers who didn't barge along the starting line or utter terrifying shrieks when the starter's gun went off.

But the competition became more intense as August waned. Now, in addition to Mr. Gulden and his grandchildren, we also had *Juno,* Susan John's 26-foot Zephyr skippered by my old nemesis Jack Slatterly. Two other Timber Points also joined the August races, and so did another sloop I had never seen before, a Shinnecock from West Hampton, a cross between the Timber Point and the Zephyr—not as sleek as the former or as beamy as the latter.

The August races were, in fact, tuneups for the traditional Labor Day competition sponsored by the Islip Boat Club, which attracted sloops from all along the south shore. After this one final race, I vowed that I would never race again. But I decided not to mention this to Martin, who said, "I think we can win, provided we don't lose a rudder."

"Or our heads," I added, thinking mostly of myself.

As usual I was worried about the quality of the wind.

236

What I wanted was a southwest breeze that picked up to eight knots or so by early afternoon, raising an occasional whitecap in the distance, like the hoary wing of a herring gull, glimpsed for an instant on the crest of a wave. That was the kind of wind *Circe* and I had come to understand. It was the wind of moderation, not so light that it impeded motion and not so strong that we had to plunge constantly into the oncoming waves.

I was aware that every other skipper on the bay had his own special wind too. I suspected that the owners of the other Timber Points rigged differently from *Circe* (they had long booms and short masts, while *Circe* had a short boom and a long mast) would prefer a stiffer breeze. Ten knots seemed to be a dividing line: under ten knots *Circe* pointed higher and over ten knots they pointed higher. But it also occured to me that it wasn't so much the rig of the sloop as the temperament of the helmsman that dictated such preferences. I was a helmsman with a penchant for a moderate breeze.

My gods were with us that Labor Day. The sky was filled with fleeting, wispy horsetails, not dense enough to block the sun that warmed the land. The onshore breeze picked up at ten in the morning, stiffened to six knots at noon and climbed to nine knots with Captain Plunkett's warning gun. The wind was brisk but not so stiff as to raise a Bay chop to pound against the hulls.

Captain Plunkett had set a long, two-legged course—ten miles out to windward and then a run for home—that would occupy the contenders, about forty boats split into two divisions, through the afternoon. The starting line, as usual, was off Bayberry Point, Islip. From there the boats would beat upwind until they

237

reached the State Boat Channel off Babylon, where they would round a marker and fly with the wind astern back to where they began.

As we jockeyed for position around the starting line, I saw the stubby *Nimrod* off to leeward, with my aunt and uncle aboard. They had come to follow the race. I put them out of my mind; I knew exactly where I wanted to be. But the white-hulled Shinnecock had tacked in front of us and blocked our way. We ran away from the starting line, jibed and headed back again. We crossed ten seconds after the gun went off fairly high to windward, but not high enough.

Somehow Gulden had slipped in at the last minute and taken the windward position. The Shinnecock crossed the line ahead of Gulden, but slightly to leeward. We crossed the line even with the Shinnecock but even farther to leeward. Slats, steering *Juno* with Susan Johns as his crew, had decided to avoid the strife at the high end of the starting line. He crossed ahead of all of us, his wind clear but considerably to leeward. Obviously he was counting on his superior upwind helmsmanship to gain the windward position once the race was underway.

The other two Timber Points crossed at the high end of the line too, but they were late and lagging. The race would be settled among the four of us: Gulden, the Shinnecock, Slats and *Circe*.

The Shinnecock couldn't point as high into the wind as *Circe*—that was evident at once. After a hundred yards we tacked behind her, but I was certain we'd be well ahead if our paths should cross again.

Seeing *Circe* tack, Gulden tacked too, to cover us; but we were also pointing higher than he. After a quarter mile, when we were slightly astern but well to windward, Gulden made his second tack, heading straight for us, but he couldn't clear our bow.

"Starboard! Starboard!" Martin shrieked, as if he had been waiting all his life to shout those words at a millionaire. But Gulden, always the gentleman, knew we had the right of way and he crossed our wake. I was about to tack to cover Gulden when Martin shouted that Slats was also driving straight for us about a hundred yards away.

I assumed that Slats, on a port tack, would come about before he reached us, since we remained on the starboard tack and had the right of way. But he held to his collision course without swerving, exhibiting an arrogance that infuriated me.

"What's he think he's doing!" Martin said.

"He's bluffing. He thinks we'll fall off and let him cross our bow!"

"Well, he's got another think coming!" Martin said. Kneeling on the foredeck, he waved his arms furiously and shouted: "Starboard, starboard, starboard . . . ," the word tumbling out and traveling over the water above the swish of the converging hulls. I refused to give, and if Slats failed to come about then *Juno*'s sharp prow would ram us amidships.

Undaunted, Slats came as close as he dared, then abruptly came about, cutting his momentum. As his sails filled on the other side, we swooped down and stole his wind, so that his sails emptied and luffed again. He knew it was coming and so did Susan Johns—I could tell by the expression on her face. I was tempted to shout as we swept by, "I owed you that one, Slats—from a long time ago!" But I didn't want him to know I remembered, and so I acted simply as though I were engaged in the everyday tactics of a sailboat race.

Martin let out a whoop as we flew by under full wind-power while *Juno* had to gather herself together again. I settled on the lee side of the boat, the way the captain had taught me, with the tiller over my shoulder, holding it gently between forefinger and thumb. I let my sloop climb the wind of her own volition; when the jib luffed slightly I eased off and then let her climb again. Within a few minutes we were positioned favorably, well to windward of the other sloops. Gulden was our nearest competitior. Every time the mustard tycoon came about, Martin would tell me and we'd do the same.

I didn't see the other boats on that windward leg; I wasn't aware of the passage of time. Every now and then Martin would tell me that we were "pulling ahead, pulling ahead," but I didn't really care. I was exhilarated not by the race but by the mystical link between me and the sloop as she sliced through the sea. I was sailing now with a sense of grace I had never known before.

As we rounded the first mark ahead of the others, I heard Captain Hubbard's voice boom across the water. "Raise the spinnaker, ya darn fool!" Martin sprang to the forward deck; soon the great sail billowed before us as we boiled along with the wind behind. We crossed the finish line first and won the race by seconds on corrected time. The second boat was a Snipe that I didn't even know was there.

For that feat we received a trophy of anodized gold with a bronze inscription that tarnished with time. But the sweet taste of that triumph remained with me months afterward.

That fall I left for an inland college amid the rolling hills of upstate New York. On bitter nights, before I slept, I would recollect that summer day I sailed my sloop upwind in a brisk breeze. I would see *Nimrod* to leeward and Martin Newcomb, faithful friend, prone on the windward deck. But I was aware only of the tiller between my fingers and thumb, and the surge of the blue sloop as she climbed the wind.

11 ⌒

I had no qualms about going off to college. I felt I had been on my own since my parents died. From sailing I had learned resourcefulness. I could accept what was given; I could adapt, I could prevail. But now alienation afflicted me like a dread disease. My roots were in my homelessness, for I hadn't yet found that place where I belonged. I could sleep as easily in a dormitory as in my bedroom under the eaves—perhaps even more so, for in the dormitory I didn't have to contend with those emotional undertows that rip through family life.

The Union College campus was an oasis amid the industrial city of Schenectady. Quiet walkways bordered by towering elms and a hodgepodge of colonial and classical buildings (including a bizarre domed library with 16 ivy-covered sides) blended gracefully into the peaceful setting. One entered the campus through a wrought-iron gate that bore a plaque stating that the college had been founded in 1795. I could feel tradition in my bones. I settled into a commodious room in North College that overlooked 17 acres of sunken gardens split by the gur-

242

gling Hans Groot kill. The College was a place of study and solitude, my first real home.

Sara had no such refuge. She had departed for a New England university two years earlier and returned within the week, lonely and homesick. Of course, that's not what she said. She said her dormitory was dirty, infested with roaches, and her roommates were vulgar and foul-mouthed. Instead of sending her straight back, Aunt Flo and Uncle Bert sympathized and sheltered her. The truth was that they missed her as much as she missed them; they couldn't exist without the endless bickering she inspired.

They let her enroll in a commuter college and live at home. But they lost her anyhow. In her junior year she met and married a young man named George Maltbie, who was majoring in business administration. An amiable, nondescript individual, Maltbie harnessed himself to Sara's drive and went to work for Uncle Bert after his graduation. And so the Manns got their daughter back, except now the internecine warfare encompassed the business as well as the home.

By then it was well established that I wouldn't join Uncle Bert's firm, even though his business boomed during the postwar years. I had neither the interest nor the aptitude for title search and mortgage guaranty. I was going to be a poet and support myself chasing fire engines for the *Bay Shore Sentinel*, where Vic Scanlon put me to work writing stories and editing copy whenever I came home from Schenectady. Aunt Flo informed me that I couldn't support a family that way. I told her I had no intention of supporting a family.

"That's what you say now," she said. "Well, we'll see."

I revelled in my independence: I was a man apart, estranged; the entire earth was my home and I was free to roam the world. Of course the money I earned working for Vic Scanlon wasn't much, but it was enough to buy a ticket to a faraway country, provided I travelled alone. So I decided to put *Circe* up on drydock and spend the following summer in Mexico.

Except before I could leave the bay, I had to put an end to an onerous love: the sweet goddess Margery Hubbard whom I'd pursued through all those painful years. I adored her in high school; I became so preoccupied with her that I had no time for any other girl. But by the time I entered college my adoration had abated, and she had dwindled to an innocuous habit, a pallid novel I couldn't lay aside. Adoration, I had discovered, isn't the stuff from which passionate love is made. Once I had worshipped *Circe* too, from afar; but after she became mine and I learned the feel of her, my adoration passed.

But Margery wasn't hull and keel; she was flesh and bone. I thought that if I could only get close enough to touch her I could root her forever from my heart and mind. But she was too elusive and ethereal. All through my youth I had this image of Margery waving gaily at me across the water and then, as I neared, slipping away.

She went off to college the same time I did, and we wrote to each other regularly. I looked ahead to Christmas vacation, and when I arrived home I called her every day. Sometimes she would see me and sometimes she wouldn't, depending on her mood. Regardless, I would walk to her house and visit with her father. The captain spent the long winter sitting in front of a tiny television

244

set, watching "the wrasslin' matches." I saw a lot of "wrasslin' " and very little of Margery during that holiday.

Then one glum December afternoon toward the end of the year (just as Jumbo Jake was tightening his toehold on Devil Dan) a blue convertible pulled up outside the Hubbard home and an athletic young man bounded up to the front door. All at once Margery came flying out of her upstairs bedroom, down the stairs and into his arms. She introduced me to her boyfriend as if I were one of her father's cronies who had stopped by to chat about the good old sailing days on the Great South Bay.

So that was it—she had a lover, someone she had met at college and who had driven heaven knew how far to feel the warmth of her body against his own. I watched the two of them skip out the front door, arm in arm, and drive away.

For a long while I felt nothing at all. Then gradually I was overcome with a pleasant sensation, a mild euphoria, as if I had finally put a great burden down and could now walk upright once again. It wasn't until I returned to college that I identified this feeling as one of relief. I went to my desk and composed a narrative poem, the words forming on the paper more rapidly than in my head. The poem was about my imaginary affair with the daughter of a charter boat captain. It sketched the course of our idyllic love, month by month, through a single eventful calendar year. In the summer we sailed and in the fall we picked apples and in the winter we snuggled up to the fire in a cozy room. That sort of thing. At the end of the poem a mysterious stranger drops from the sky while the lovers are strolling along a deserted beach and tells them they will no longer be permitted to live in a vacuum:

> *. . . and the man who had dropped from the sky*
> *and raced across the beach like a hobo*
> *walked up the beach in a mourning suit*
> *and drove away in a black car*
> *and I looked for the captain's daughter*
> *who had gone somewhere else*
> *someplace where . . .*

At first I called it "A Funny Poem"; later I changed the title to "The End of a Romantic Affair", which was a presumption since there had never been such an affair. I submitted it to *The Idol*, the college literary magazine, and a few days later Howie Simons, the editor, told me he was going to publish it in the center spread.

A month later, when I received the galley proofs to check, I was dismayed by what I saw and stormed into Simons' room. I had written the poem with a small "i" in the style of e.e. cummings and Simons had changed all my first person pronouns from lower to upper case without my permission.

"You can't do that!" I thundered. "You have no right!"

He measured me calmly. "For Cummings, it's fine," he said. "For you, it's an affectation."

"Either publish it the way I wrote it," I said, "or don't publish it at all!"

He backed off and reset the type.

The Idol appeared with my poem on a prematurely warm spring day before the elms bloomed. I sat on the library steps and read it through three times. I was puzzled by the man in the mourning suit who dropped from the sky and drove away in a black car. Who was he? Was I still bedeviled by death?

Then I realized the mysterious stranger wasn't death; he was life. He had dropped from nowhere and stolen the goddess away and set me free. I was rid of her once and for all.

It was a good poem, but it was better therapy.

Liberated at last, I began to cast about with a vengeance for other girls, as if I had already wasted a lifetime. That spring I had tried out for an acting part with the Mountebanks, the college dramatic society, and won the role of Salanio, a minor character in *The Merchant of Venice*. I was smitten at once with Jessica, Shylock's daughter. A seductive Jewess, Jessica paraded around the stage in a white wraparound gown that revealed her cleavage. Dark complected and clearly passionate, she twirled on a high stool in the wings while waiting for her cues. I had to force myself to look the other way. Finally I cornered her behind the backdrop during dress rehearsal while Bassanio was soliloquizing about why he was going to pick a chest of dross instead of silver or gold to win fair Portia's hand.

"Say," I whispered to Jessica, "what are you doing Saturday night?"

"I'm terribly sorry, Salanio," she said, "but I'm already engaged."

I was as disappointed as Portia's numerous wooers before Bassanio came along, but I persevered. I approached Portia, the lady lawyer, and became one of her rejected suitors myself. Finally I received an affirmative response from Nerissa, Portia's maid, a dowdy girl with a freckled face, but not altogether unappealing. One night I walked her along the old Erie Barge Canal that threaded under moonlight beside the city. Standing on its murky shores, I declaimed:

> *In such a night*
> *Stood Dido with a willow in her hand*
> *Upon the wild sea-banks, and waft her love*
> *To come again to Carthage.*

I was hoping the bard's familiar pentameters would work their magic on her heart. She recognized those forlorn lines uttered by a desperate lover and said, "I'm sick to death of that stupid play."

Meanwhile I had to contend with the college athletic director who was determined to harrass me. After opening night he came backstage, ostensibly to congratulate the members of the cast, but when he saw me he said: "Bode, what's a big guy like you doing in frilly Elizabethan pants?"

I had blundered. When I was accepted at the college I unwittingly filled out a form declaring that I had been an all-county end in high school and played varsity basketball and baseball as well. Since Union didn't award athletic scholarships, the coaches were interested in any student who could catch a ball without bending a finger. The football coach actually called me at home and invited me to college two weeks early to try out for the football team. It was an honor and he was taken aback when I refused. I told him the fairest summer winds were yet to come and I had too many races to sail. Fortunately, the football team had a glut of ends that year. Nevertheless, the athletic director was still bent upon luring me back to the fields of play.

Sara's first child, a son, was born that spring. I went to the college bookstore and purchased a copy of Stevenson's *A Child's Garden of Verses* for the infant. It was a sincere gesture on my part. What better way to wean a child on words than with those lilting verses with their vivid imagery. But I learned from Aunt Flo that Sara was put off by my gift.

"What good is a book?" she said. "He can't read." I had unwittingly committed an act of ingratitude. Better I had bought a rattle with a pacifier on the end.

And so I made a special trip home to visit Sara in her new house and to study this wondering child, with its tiny arms and legs, who gazed wide-eyed about the room. I concluded they were all wrong. I read one of Stevenson's verses to him, and he looked at me, knowingly.

"Tommy, that's your Uncle Rick," Sara said, and her words sounded strange. I was an uncle.

"How do you know he can't read?" I said to Sara. "He looks bright enough to me." She wasn't amused.

I left Sara's and went to Anson's shipyard. It was early May and the wind was from the south. For months I had known nothing except the arid inland smell of winter hills, bare and burning in the nostrils, but now the pungent aroma from the tidal bogs filled my soul with expectancy. The boat cover was folded back and the breeze was billowing under the canvas, blowing along *Circe*'s musty deck.

"Haloo Rick!"

"Haloo Simmy!"

"I opened her up," he said, as he came toward me from the Ballyhoo. "Give the deck a chance to breathe."

"Thanks, Simmy."

"Ready to go to work?"

"I can't Simmy. I have to go back for final exams, and as soon as they're over I'm leaving for Mexico."

"Mexico!" Simmy rubbed his hand along the side of his leathery face. "That's not so good," he said. "I don't like to see her laying up on dry dock, her boards shrinking that way, all summer long."

"Can we fill her up with water from the inside?" I asked.

"I don't care much for that idea," he said. "It puts too much weight on the wrong side of the hull." He rubbed the stubble on his chin and squinted at the sun. "I'll tell you what. Suppose I scrub and paint her bottom for you. Then Howie and I can launch her so she swells. If I get a chance I'll put a coat of varnish on them decks too. Then when you come back she'll be ready to go."

I hesitated.

"Hey," he said, "don't worry about the cost! It's repayment for all them free punctuation marks you've supplied me through the years. I'll do it one Saturday morning when Roy Anson isn't around. Roy's losing interest in the place. He doesn't seem to care much about anything anymore."

"Simmy," I said, "you're a friend."

"Mexico!" he harrumphed, as if he couldn't imagine who had put that crazy notion into my head.

I had a Ford coupe, an overpowered eight-cylinder perpetual motion machine that had already served Uncle Bert for ten years, chugging back and forth between his house in Brightwaters and the railroad station in Bay Shore. Shortly after I left for college, he took an apartment in the city (using the house only for winter weekends and a summer retreat) and gave his battered but trustworthy station car to me. It had a standard shift with a balky clutch that caused the car to buck like a bronco if the driver didn't understand the eccentricities of its gears. There was no radio or heater, but it had two taxi seats that flopped down in the back and, for ventilation, a gaping hole in the floor. Its body was aging but its engine was strong. On the morning after my last exam, I shoved a suitcase into its sloping trunk and headed south and west toward Mexico.

I slept in towns with strange sounding names: Pulaski, Virginia, and Lebanon, Tennessee. In Little Rock, I indulged myself with a warm bath in the best hotel, and then I hugged the arrow-straight road across the limitless Texas prairie all the way to Laredo on the Rio Grande. There I put my car in a garage and bought a bus ticket for Mexico City, still 600 hundred miles away. I had left Schenectady with four hundred dollars in my pocket; three hundred I'd earned myself and Uncle Bert had contributed another hundred (unbeknownst to Aunt Flo) on the sly. I was determined to stretch it out, make it last into September if I could. I had already explored the streets of Washington, Memphis and San Antonio. I had crossed the Mississippi for the first time. And I'd covered 2000 miles in seven days, long before the network of interstate highways made such journeys routine.

On a cloudless morning the fiery ball rose and blazed across the desert sky. The rickety bus departed two hours late, which, by local standards, was right on time. Besides myself, there were only three other Americans aboard: two adventurous nurses on a holiday and a pock-marked writer who said he ground out Westerns for pulp magazines. All the other passengers were Mexican, true and poor, swarthy, proud descendants of the people who possessed the land long before the Spaniards came.

On the dusty road outside Monterrey, a carabinero with a rifle slung across his shoulder halted the bus and climbed aboard. He strode down the aisle, glowering at each passenger, then stepped off and waved the driver on his way. In Ciudad Victoria, another officer stopped the bus again, seized a man slumped under a sombrero and dragged him off, as if he were to be executed on the spot.

Toward evening the jagged peaks rose behind the long shadows of the setting sun. How different from the sandy moraine that sloped so gently into the Great South Bay. What upheavals this land had known! At first the slopes were bare and somber, but soon they became lush with live green undergrowth. We fried by day as we crossed the desert; now we froze by night as the bus climbed the treacherous road into the Sierra Madres. The driver straddled the center of the narrow highway as he roared around hairpin turns, blaring his horn to warn oncoming traffic but never giving way. The villages materialized under the mountain stars; each time we stopped the children surrounded the vehicle to sell fresh fruit and beg for coins.

Toward noon of the second day the bus circled out of the clouds and Mexico City spread before us on the high plateau. I broke out in hives, which one of the nurses told me was an allergic reaction to the fruit I had eaten along the way. I took two antihistamines and fell asleep. When I awoke my itch was gone. The bus was in the depot and the pockmarked author was saying goodbye.

I went straight to the University and enrolled in two courses, conversational Spanish and the history of Spanish literature. At the housing office I obtained the address of a Mexican family with a room to rent on the third floor. It turned out to be exactly what I had hoped for. The house itself, built of an adobe-like concrete, was on a narrow side street off the glorious Paseo de la Reforma. The room literally sat on the roof, like a penthouse, overlooking the courtyard. In the distance I could see the Bosque Chapultepec and Maximilian's Castle.

I shared this room with one Carlos Parra y Corral, nephew of the widowed owner and a student like myself though somewhat older. Carlos had a powerful, stocky build and a carefree attitude. He had received a scholarship to Columbia University several years earlier, but he couldn't accept. "If I went," he said in his flawless English, "your country would have drafted me and sent me off to war." So he stayed in Mexico. He seemed to have no regrets and he never went to class, as far as I could see.

That first night Carlos took me to the jai alai matches where he tossed away fifty pesos (at eight pesos to the dollar) of my precious store of cash by betting on both sides at the same time. But I didn't care; I was alive and emboldened by this vivid land. Later he took me through the Palacio de las Bellas Artes with its gleaming walls and yellow domes. There I saw the bold frescoes of Rivera and Orozco, tendentious and romantic, works that could only have been created by artists steeped in the lore of this country where the colors clashed and the classes warred.

Behind the Palacio we wandered through the red-light district. A whore darted out of a hovel and grabbed me. Carlos laughed and chased her away. "If you want a woman," he said to me afterward, "don't come here. You ask me first. I know where there are better girls. I will take you there sometime."

On the way home, we saw a troubadour singing under a balcony to a young woman who listened with her hands folded across her breast.

Each morning I would stroll through Chapultepec to the zoo and there sit under a giant ahuehuete tree and watch the rowers in the lake. The mornings were always sparkling, but by early afternoon the dark clouds would suddenly blow across the city and rain would drench the streets. Then, all at once, the clouds would disappear and the sun would shine again.

In the late morning I would take a bus to the university and sit through a tedious lecture that tried to explain what this country of contrasts was all about. I met a girl in my literature class who was as bored as I. She had curly yellow hair and had arrived from her home in Colorado in a brand new baby-blue convertible. Her name was Carol Linley and her father, a rancher, owned ten thousand acres of grazing land. One day she told me she was going to drive to Taxco for a long weekend to meet some friends.

"I always wanted to go to Taxco," I said.

"Well come on!" she said.

The streets of Taxco were lined with silver shops and the hollow sound of burros hooves echoed against the cobblestones. "How like the sound of caulking hammers," I thought, but there were no shipyards within a hundred miles of that rugged mountain spot. We had to leave her car outside the city and walk up a steep hill to our hotel rooms where we stayed for five days. Carol paid the bill.

"Where are your friends?" I asked.

"Oh, I guess they've slipped away."

She purchased two hundred dollars of silver trinkets for her younger sisters.

"Let's go wander about the city," I would say.

"If we must," she'd reply with a heavy sigh.

But after an hour of staring at the churches and the shops and the burros she would steer me back to the hotel.

"When the summer is over," she said, "you can come back with me to Colorado. My father will give you a job."

I had the dry taste of the desert in my mouth and I could see the endless land of gray-green sage.

"Colorado isn't my home," I said.

All at once I was filled with a longing for familiar names and scenes: Timber Point and Saltaire and the flicker of the Fire Island Light across the Captree dunes.

12 ～

It was late August when I packed my bags and headed over the mountains into the desert and across the Rio Grande. I picked up my coupe, pressed the starter button and the engine turned over as if it had been running full tilt only yesterday. I had barely enough money left to make it home. I slept in a New Orleans flophouse and on top of Lookout Mountain under the stars. I drove without stopping, except for gas, from Chattanooga to Bay Shore.

When I arrived home, I crawled into my bed under the eaves and slept for two days. When I awoke the sky was filled with a piercing light and the sea breeze was fluttering the curtains in my room. I threw my sailbag over my shoulder and went down to the shipyard where I found *Circe* tied up behind the Ballyhoo, rigged neat and trim, just as Simmy said she'd be.

I paddled across the dead spot behind the shipyard sheds until the light breeze filled my sails. I trimmed the sheets; *Circe* heeled and turned upwind. The Kismet ferry, approaching from astern, cut its engines and passed me on the lee side. Women in billowing summer

256

dresses sat along the upper deck, glancing idly over the rail. But toward the bow a small boy was watching *Circe*, the wonder in his eyes. I waved and his face lit up.

I followed the ferry's wake for nearly a mile and then left the channel for the shoals. The tide was in and I could wend my way across the flats, through the clam-bed markers along the eastern shore of Captree Island, the secret route I had learned from Ed Doubrava—was it yesterday? The wind, fresh and southerly, would shift steadily to the west as the day wore on. But now it angled exactly right for my landfall. I sailed close-hauled, the water churning over the lee rail and swirling under the hull. It was my wind, and it filled the sails and my hungry soul.

I glided past the Wa Wa Yonda Club, still forsaken, as if waiting for the weather to ravage it. But that wasn't the weather's way. The weather, the wind and rain, takes its toll a little at a time, and so the Wa Wa Yonda Club appeared the same to me that day as it had when Gwen and I roamed through it so many years before. A shudder ran through my body, the sudden chill that comes from too much joy. Nothing had changed. This was my land, my wind, my bay.

I sailed into the State Boat Channel and a great blue heron rose from the reeds and soared, alighting farther down the shore.

Beyond Captree the channel broadened. Ahead I saw the estuary that separated Oak Island from the barrier beach, and I spotted the familiar line of summer homes. I hadn't thought of sailing there. The homing pigeon doesn't think; the homing pigeon flies.

I came up to the Gowan dock, lowered the jib and

257

leaped ashore with a line. I dropped a clove hitch around the mooring post and walked along the dock to the porch in front of the Gowan summer home. Frank Gowan was asleep under his hat. Mrs. Gowan came to the screen door, a finger to her lips, and then seeing it was me, said aloud: "Land sakes, Rick Bode, I haven't seen you for years!"

Mr. Gowan woke up and we sat on the porch and chatted for a while. I told them about my trip to Mexico, but Mr. Gowan's eyes kept drifting off to the west and I knew what he was looking for. He was looking for the November sky and the flight of scaup, but they were still two months away. As for Mexico—he was a polite man, but Mexico was beyond his ken. Oak Island was his true home. Why, in this one small place he hadn't yet exhausted all the possibilities.

The Gowans were kindly people without pretension. They knew I hadn't crossed the bay to visit with them, and yet they acted as if I had. They invited me for lunch, and they didn't say a word about Gwen until I asked if she was there.

"Why no, Rick," Mrs. Gowan said. "Don't you know —she's away at nursing school."

"Oh, I guess I didn't know," I said.

Before I left, Mrs. Gowan wrote out Gwen's address and phone number at Flower Fifth Avenue Hospital in Manhattan and gave it to me. "Give her a call," she said. "I'm sure she'd like to hear from you."

I returned to the sloop and cast off. It skimmed easily along, the gentle wind behind. Although my sails were filled, my heart ached and I felt a void. I was alone at that moment when I had so much to share. "Gwen, Gwen,"

258

I said aloud, "how could you be off at nursing school when I wanted so much to find you here!"

It was one thing to make an impromptu landing at the Gowan dock in the dead of summer; it was something else to call on Gwen in a strange place—a hospital, a nursing school. I had seen her only sporadically over the years and I wasn't sure I could cope with the girl I'd find: she had such swift currents, such ever-changing moods. And so I folded the paper with her address on it, which Mrs. Gowan had given to me, and tucked it into my wallet.

I began to see that I too was a creature of caprice and mood, moved by a sense of rightness that was less learned than intuitive. I put things off until I felt the moment was suitable, but my timing wasn't governed by calculation or schedule. An inner clock, a private calendar, told me when to act and when to bide my time.

There are those who might see this as a weakness, a wavering, but I think they're wrong. Nor do I think I'm singular in this respect. Each man has his inborn sense of season that he dare not ignore. Move too soon or too late and the best of plans will go awry.

When I returned to college that fall, I met a girl who was studying design at Russell Sage in nearby Troy. She was tall, cool and aloof, and she had flaming red hair. I thought I detected a passion under her passivity. Once I picked her up on a Saturday afternoon and we drove through the Schoharie Valley, picnicking in a field by the river near Middleburg. The stream ran swiftly over the rocks and under a bridge; on the far bank the ash, oak and sugar maples had turned red and gold. Farther up the embankment the poplars shimmered in the wind and the white birch stood out boldly against the spruce. But she was indifferent to the blazing countryside. When I reached for her hand it was cold, and after that day I didn't bother with her any more.

Thanksgiving I went home—not to Brightwaters but to the apartment Uncle Bert had taken on Third Avenue beside the elevated subway, which rattled the dishes in the kitchen cupboard every time it thundered by.

The Manhattan apartment doubled Aunt Flo's woes. Now instead of having one place to clean, she had two. Uncle Bert stopped commuting and Aunt Flo began. She shuttled back and forth between her two residences with her dust mop, vacuum cleaner and assorted laundry bags, all heaped in the back seat of her sedan. Uncle Bert offered to pay for a cleaning woman, but Aunt Flo never found one who could do the job to her satisfaction. So she did it herself. She said it was a trial, but a necessary one, and she was willing to make the sacrifice.

I always tried to anticipate her moves and occupy the abode she had just left. During the long Thanksgiving weekend that year I had exceptional luck. Both Aunt Flo and Uncle Bert had decided to have a family Thanksgiving with the Maltbies in Brightwaters and they were content to let me have the apartment to myself. In truth, Aunt Flo didn't care to leave me alone in either place as she was afraid I would mess it up. She cautioned me against throwing wild parties for my carousing friends, not quite realizing how much I prized my solitary life. But in the end she decided it was easier to keep me at a reasonable distance than to put up with me. I had grown restless in a way neither she nor Uncle Bert could comprehend.

That long November weekend the Third Avenue apartment beside the "El" proved a blessing. I slept on a studio couch under the living room window not more than thirty yards from the roaring subway cars. At first they kept me awake, but after a while they became as soporific as a lullaby. The living quarters were close, but the city was vast and, for me, unexplored. I roamed the streets, visited the museums, the galleries, the theater. I hiked from the Battery to the Cloisters at Fort Tryon Park. I saw old men playing boccie under the shadow of the Williamsburg Bridge, and I watched ghettos kids shooting baskets in a caged school yard within a stone's throw of the Harlem River.

One afternoon I strolled uptown along Riverside Drive from Seventy-Second Street to Grant's Tomb. With each passing city block scenes from my childhood flashed through my mind. As I walked around the Soldiers' and Sailors' Memorial overlooking the Hudson and the distant Palisades, I recalled how I had visited that monument as a small boy, holding my father's hand. A young brigand with a slingshot was sitting on a bench, shooting slyly at pigeons and passersby, then hiding his weapon between his legs. My father, his face black, walked up to the youth. "Let's see that slingshot!" he said. As the culprit held it out, my father's hand, quick as a cobra's strike, reached out and snapped the rubber band. Then, without so much as a word, my father turned and walked away.

I remembered too how after a snowfall my father and I would glide together down the long slope that

261

stretched from the Drive to the fenced-off railroad tracks that ran beside the River. He would lie on the sled and I would lie on top of him, wrapping my arms around his neck and hanging on for dear life. We would fly together down a preliminary slope, across an icy sidewalk, and then up and over a huge bump and down, down the long hill. The ride lasted forever. Now, as I passed that site again, I noticed the park had been rearranged for a highway and the exciting bump landscaped out of existence.

I reached back in memory to find the essence of my father's character. What was he like? He was a freelance artist—that smacked of independence and a courage to face economic uncertainty. He dared live—I knew that from his romantic paintings that bespoke a man who yearned for beauty. I realized then that I too would have to make my separate way through life, not from alienation but from choice. All at once I felt a kinship with my father; I gathered in his strength, and in that instant I felt a sudden joy, as though my time had come.

I turned eastward and crossed the northern edge of Central Park. A few blocks south—and I was standing in front of Flower Fifth Avenue Hospital, an old gray stone building in which I shouldn't have cared to be confined had I been ill. I went to a pay telephone in the lobby and removed Gwen's number from my wallet. My heart was pounding fiercely.

I heard a girl's voice over the wire, shouting down the hall. "Where's Gwen? Is Gwen here? Tell her she has a call! Some guy!" After an unconscionably long time Gwen came to the phone.

"Gwen, I would like to see you."

"Well, when?"

262

"Right now!"

"Where are you?"

"Downstairs."

I went up to the third floor and sat in a waiting room with stiff chairs. After a while Gwen came in wearing a light green student's uniform. She was Gwen—yes, but I could see she had changed too. She had those same steely eyes that seemed to penetrate objects, whether translucent or opaque. But a good deal of definition had come into the lines of her face, which was appealing to me because it was so strong and plain. She held herself back, aloof and proud, and I couldn't tell if she was glad to see me or not.

"Rick," she said, "I don't have much time. I'm on duty and my supervisor will kill me if she finds out I'm missing for long."

We talked a few minutes, and as she started to leave I said, "Gwen, there's going to be a dance at college just before the Christmas holidays. Will you come up to Schenectady?"

She looked at me evenly for what seemed a long time and then said, with some effort I thought, "No, I don't think so."

"But Gwen, why not?"

"Rick, I have to run. Call me before you come next time. Give me a chance."

I was hurt, more devastated than I could remember. She was treating me as if I were a stranger, someone she hardly knew. She had said "no" to me. How could she say "no" to me? How could she be so cruel!

I returned to Union, but for a week I couldn't study, I couldn't concentrate. The image of Gwen kept whirling through my mind. Whenever I called her long distance she was on duty. I thought perhaps she had another boy, but that didn't worry me. If she had another I would compete with him and and if he then won at least I would know I hadn't lost by default.

Finally, one night I got her on the phone.

"Gwen," I said, "why did you say 'no'?"

"Because I figured if you couldn't go to that dance with the girl who was your first choice, you shouldn't go at all."

"But Gwen, you are my first choice!"

"Well, the way you popped in here so unexpectedly like that—it's as if I were just an afterthought."

I could see then how my impromptu actions troubled her. Whenever we'd met in the past, it had always been by happenstance and never design.

"Gwen, you're hardly an afterthought. I haven't asked anyone else. I'm asking you, only you."

She was silent for a moment and I could hear her catch her breath.

"Why didn't you say that right away?"

My heart sang. "Then you'll come?"

No," she said, "I can't. Honestly, Rick, I would if I could. But this place is like a prison and I can't get away that weekend."

"Gwen," I said, "that's all right. I understand that, I really do. If you can't come up here, I'll come down there. When you have time off we'll take a walk together through the park or along the river. Can we do that?"

"Of course—but, really, I won't mind if you ask somebody else."

264

Did she mean that, or was it a test? If it was the latter, I wasn't going to fail.

"Gwen," I said, "if I can't go to that dance with the girl who is my first choice, I'd rather not go at all."

The following summer and the next, Gwen and I sailed together whenever we could. After completing three years of training, she began to work in a local hospital. During my summer vacations I worked nights for the Macy chain of newspapers in Suffolk County. We had our days off in the middle of the week, the best time, for that was when the bay and the beaches were deserted.

Gwen had no great desire to handle the sloop; she left the sailing to me. If I told her to trim a sheet, she trimmed a sheet; if I told her to fend off, she fended off, and if I told her to throw an anchor overboard, she did that too. But she preferred to lie on the forward deck, turning herself over slowly so she baked evenly. She would lie flat on her back with a boat cushion under her head while the spray brushed her face and the droplets glistened on her skin. If the jib was trimmed to port, she would lie high on the starboard deck, and when we'd come about she would grudgingly shift to the other side. Or she would lie face down on the cushion and fall asleep, lulled by the sound of the water rushing past the hull as *Circe* sliced through the sea.

While she drowsed I would sit contentedly in the cockpit, tiller over my shoulder, glancing up at the jib and down at her. I marvelled at the way her body conformed to the sheer of the deck, as if she and the sloop had been

265

struck from a common mold. Once, when she lay sleeping, the breeze picked up a knot or two. I trimmed the sheet so that *Circe* heeled sharply and she rolled overboard into the bay. I headed into the wind and she swam to the stern with clean, strong strokes. I fished her out, wet and furious, into my arms.

But on another occasion she slipped on the wet deck and fell backwards, striking the base of her spine on a cleat. I was filled with dread; the way she moaned and writhed I thought she had cracked a bone. But it was only a bruise, although it was a long time before she could sit comfortably again. She sprawled prone on the windward deck.

"How does it feel?"

"Not so bad."

"I could rub it for you."

"That won't be necessary."

I rubbed it anyhow, letting my hands wander over her back.

"That's not where it hurts," she said.

We sailed to every part of the bay we knew so well, and I had a sense of completeness I'd never felt before. I sailed with a knowledge that had become second nature, with a woman who was at home and took pleasure in what I saw. A great calmness possessed her, like the vast stillness of the sea; and yet, like the sea, she had a latent power and might, without warning, rage.

Some days we sailed westward to her parent's summer house on Oak Island; other days we sailed eastward to Great River. We sailed by the Moorish houses on Bayberry Point and skirted the treacherous shoals at Fire Island Inlet where once, with Ed Doubrava, I had dug so many clams. We would set out in the morning and catch the freshening breeze before the whitecaps appeared.

"Where to today, Lady Gwendolyn?"

"Why don't you just tack out of this canal and see what strikes your fancy?"

And that's exactly what we'd do.

Late one afternoon Gwen decided she wanted to troll for bluefish while we were sailing home. She infuriated me. She knew I didn't like to fish and sail at the same time. I was afraid of the fishing line getting snagged in the sheets. And then there was always the half-alive fish flopping around the cockpit while I was trying to steer. I tried to put her off.

"It's kind of late, isn't it?"

"See," she said, "the tide is changing. The blues are here. I can see them jumping."

"But the tide is ebbing."

She thrust out her jaw. "I want to fish!"

"Darnit, Gwen, you're like a pregnant woman with a craving."

"I want to fish. Steer into the shoals. I'll get out the bait box and net."

We always sailed with her rod and reel, plus a bait box and net for trapping minnows. They were stowed under the cuddy but they were forever falling off their hooks and rolling around. "This is a sailboat," I muttered, "not a fishing skiff," but she pretended she didn't hear.

I sailed to the lee side of West Island, raised my centerboard and headed toward the shoals. Despite the late

267

hour the wind was still blowing strongly, but on the protected side of the island there were virtually no waves. The air was warm and the sun was riding down the western sky. I deliberately skimmed a sand bar, thinking to myself: "Serves her right if we run aground and get stuck out here all night!" And then that idle notion, born of petulance, became an irresistible idea. Gwen flipped the anchor overboard as I lowered the jib, letting the mainsail luff. *Circe* swung up into the wind with only a few inches of water under her keel.

We spread the net, each taking an end, and waded into the tepid water, which was slightly above our knees. If Gwen had had her wits about her she would have remembered the tide was ebbing, but she had bluefish on her mind. With the first sweep of the net we scooped up enough minnows for our purposes, but I insisted we make another sweep, just to be on the safe side. The tide was ebbing rapidly now, exposing the bars. I kept Gwen's back to the sloop so she couldn't see the keel was scraping bottom now.

"I think we have enough minnows," she said after the second sweep. I agreed, but I suggested we tread for clams. "If we don't get blues, we can drift for fluke."

"Good thought," she said, clearly pleased that I had stopped making a fuss.

Using our toes, we dug a handful of cherrystones out of the sand. Then she turned toward *Circe* and I heard her say: "Oh no!" The sloop was high and hard up on the shoals, listing slightly. "Hurry," she said, "maybe we can still push her off!"

I went on treading nonchalantly for one last clam. "It's no use," I said. "We'll never get her off until the tide turns. It looks as if we're stuck here for the night."

She wheeled, that defiant light I knew so well rising in her eyes. She waded toward me, her head tilted, her lower lip pushed out. I was watching both her hands, for I didn't know which one would deliver the roundhouse blow. But when she was directly in front of me she put her arm around my neck and pressed her forehead against mine.

"You did that deliberately, didn't you?" she said. "You knew how fast the tide was running, and you knew *Circe* would be hopelessly aground."

I slipped my hand under her knees and lifted her into my arms.

"Why are you carrying me?" she said.

"Because I don't want you to get your feet wet," I replied.

That night we built a bonfire on the deserted island and cooked some flounder and two dozen clams. Occasionally we'd see the light of a passing power boat. We both knew someone would tow us off the sandy bottom if we hailed them, but we were reconciled to spending the night as castaways.

I awoke toward morning and felt the sloop rise on the incoming tide and float free. I lowered myself into the water, pulled the boat toward the channel and dropped the anchor again in firm sand. Clambering back aboard I sat on deck, watching Gwen, waiting for the light of day. The sun didn't rise, but the rim of the earth fell away, tinging the purple clouds with red. In that dawning I beheld the girl and woman who was rooted in my life and memory. She was restive as the wind, even in her sleep; but I knew the

269

wind and I wasn't afraid to love her any more.

As I raised the sails that billowed in the freshening breeze, Gwen sat up and rubbed her eyes. By then we were thrusting through the bay, heading north toward land.

Shortly after I graduated college, Gwen and I were married in a church whose steeple I often used as a landmark while sailing the bay. By then she was a registered nurse and I was editor of the *Islip Press,* a weekly in the Macy newspaper chain. I was a journalist, covering government and politics, exposing illicit connections between politicians and homebuilders. I was stirring up scandals and investigations; I was making my way. Between the two of us there was enough income, even a chance to save; but when Gwen became pregnant I knew I would have to find a better paying newspaper job. But where? In all likelihood I would have to leave the Great South Bay.

We lived on the ground floor of a rambling Victorian house about a quarter-mile down a tree-lined street from Anson's boatyard. On summer evenings the fading salt-wind billowed the curtains that covered floor-to-ceiling windows set in the bowed end of the living room. Outside that window was a small garden of zinnias and dahlias, which Gwen tended and which attracted swallowtails and honey bees. In the final weeks of her pregnancy, she would often sit there in the window, knitting and reading at the same time, her fingers deftly maneuvering the needles, her eyes glued to the printed page.

She had made the curtains and decorated the apartment, hanging the oil paintings I had inherited from my father on the living room wall.

We didn't sail during those final months of Gwen's pregnancy. I was too busy and she was too uncomfortable. Every morning I checked *Circe* at her mooring post, however, and pumped her out each time it rained. But for the first time I began to feel the sloop was an encumbrance.

The baby was two weeks late. One evening I packed Gwen into the Ford coupe and drove her back and forth over the bumpy railroad grade crossing near the station.

"What are you trying to do?" she said.

"I'm trying to shake him loose."

"Well, you can't do it that way!"

At last the pains began. They started slowly and they stopped.

"False labor," the doctor said.

Finally the labor pains began in earnest and the doctor said to bring her in. Once she was admitted, her pains intensified, then stopped, then started again.

The doctor tried to calm me down. "Nothing to worry about," he said. "She has enough room to bear a cow. The baby's in good position. She just can't seem to get enough push."

That evening, my nerves frayed, I checked *Circe* and noticed she had shipped more water than I wished. She was sitting below her waterline from the excess weight. I pumped her dry and told myself that after the baby was born I would have Anson's haul her out to find the leak. All the next day I made a constant circuit from *Circe* to the hospital to work and back to *Circe* again. The sloop kept filling with water and I kept pumping her out.

The following morning Gwen was wheeled into the delivery room. When they wheeled her out I expected to find her pale and drawn, but her face was full, her eyes bright and she was exuberant.

"It's a boy," she called when she saw me, her hoarse voice carrying down the hall.

"I know, I know. The nurse said he's strong."

She laughed. "That's what nurses always say."

Soon she dozed off and I went home. I hadn't slept for two days. The instant I dropped backwards onto the mattress, the phone rang. It was Vic Scanlon.

"Rick," he said, "I just received a call from the police."

"Oh Vic," I said, "I can't chase after a police story now. I'm beat."

"It's not a story, Rick. It's that sloop of yours. The police say she's sunk."

"Sunk!"

"They say she's lying on the bottom right beside her mooring post."

I had to hire a dredging firm to raise the sloop and pump her out. Then Simmy came around in the shipyard launch and towed her to Anson's. She was hauled out and Oscar Boehme rebuilt the garboard planks where keel and hull meet on both port and starboard sides. I kept thinking of my promise to Jed: I had told him I would keep her up, not let her fall into disrepair, and I had let her sink at her berth.

"It's not your fault, young fella," Oscar said to me. "Those planks never did fit quite right," and he pulled a wad of oakum out of the garboard seam. "Sooner or later all this caulking stuff was bound to work out, and then she would ship water faster than you could pump her dry."

The planks Oscar shaped fit perfectly, and I set to work, with help from Simmy, to sand down and bleach the deck. It was hard work, and particularly so because I knew I wasn't doing it for myself.

"I think we'd best sell her," I told Gwen. "She's too much trouble and we don't have enough money to keep her up." I was thinking about the cost of mooring and winter storage, and soon she'd need another suit of sails.

I went to see old man Anson and found him talking in his office to a group of men in city clothes who had driven up in a Cadillac. I told him I wanted to put *Circe* on the market and he said he would try to sell it for me.

Simmy intercepted me as I was about to leave the yard. "Did you see those men Roy is talking to in there?"

"Yes, I did."

"They're investors," he said. "They're taking over the place. They're going to put in aluminum sheds and automatic overhead cranes and new winches and all the rest." Simmy shook his head. "Rick," he said sadly, "they don't know a stem from a stern."

"Simmy, what will you do?"

"Oh, don't trouble about me. Me and Wes will be shucking oysters over at Captain Bill's and living upstairs in a room over the bar." His life was changing, and mine was changing too.

One late September day, when I came home from work, I found two men sitting on the front porch, waiting for me. They said they were space salesmen from a **publishing** company, and they wanted to buy the boat together and sail it on Long Island Sound, where they lived.

"We figure she's a good boat for the Sound," one of them said.

"She's got a good lead keel," I said, "so she should handle well in the deeper water you have over there." I wanted to tell them that the sailing was better by far on the south shore where the wind came off the ocean, but I kept my peace.

"She's got a cracked rib," one of them said.

"She sank at her mooring recently," I said, "I'll tell you that. But I've had new garboard planks put in by the best mechanic hereabouts and he never breathed a word about cracked ribs. She's perfectly seaworthy, and I think you're wrong about the ribs."

"We'll offer you seven hundred and fifty dollars," the other one said.

"You'll never get her around to Long Island Sound with an offer like that."

"What are you asking?"

"Twelve hundred and fifty," I said. I was determined to return Uncle Bert's original investment, if I possibly could.

"We'll go to a thousand."

"Twelve fifty, firm!"

"Can we come and get her next weekend?"

"She'll be all set."

Gwen and I arrived before they did. Gwen was holding Jeff up to her shoulder and he was studying Simmy's leathery face and squinting at the sunlight that glinted off the rails. The yard was practically deserted. It was still too early to haul most of the boats; the owners wanted to eke out the last full measure of Indian summer before admitting another season had drawn to a close. We sat on the bottom of an upside-down dory until a skiff came into the yard and the two buyers stepped ashore.

"All set?" I asked.

"All set," they said and we made our exchange. They tied *Circe* to the stern of their power boat, swung a wide arc across the creek and headed toward the bay. I watched until *Circe* passed behind one of Anson's rickety sheds and disappeared. I had gone from death to birth and made a place of my own. Simmy thought he knew what was passing through my mind.

"Well, Rick," he said, "I guess you got your money's worth out of her."

"Yes, Simmy," I said. "I believe I did."